D0561117

DATE DUE

MAR 3 0 1995	

JOHN LE CARRÉ

Modern Critical Views

These and other titles in preparation

Modern Critical Views

JOHN LE CARRÉ

Edited and with an introduction by
Harold Bloom
Sterling Professor of the Humanities
Yale University

CHELSEA HOUSE PUBLISHERS ◇ 1987
New York ◇ New Haven ◇ Philadelphia

© 1987 by Chelsea House Publishers, a division
of Chelsea House Educational Communications, Inc.,
95 Madison Avenue, New York, NY 10016
345 Whitney Avenue, New Haven, CT 06511
5014 West Chester Pike, Edgemont, PA 19028

Introduction © 1987 by Harold Bloom

Printed and bound in the United States of America

∞ The paper used in this publication meets the minimum
requirements of the American National Standard for Permanence
of Paper for Printed Library Materials, Z39.48–1984.

Library of Congress Cataloging-in-Publication Data
John le Carré.
   Bibliography: p.
   Includes index.
   Summary: A selection of criticism, arranged in
chronological order of publication, devoted to the
fiction of John le Carré.
   1. Le Carré, John, 1931–   —Criticism and
interpretation.   2. Spy stories, English—History and
criticism.   [1. Le Carré, John, 1931–   —Criticism
and interpretation.   2. English literature—History
and criticism]   I. Bloom, Harold.   II. Series.
PR6062.E33Z73   1987   823'.914   86–31026
ISBN 0–87754–703–3 (alk. paper)

Contents

Editor's Note

This book brings together the best criticism available upon the fiction of John le Carré. The essays and reviews are arranged in the chronological order of their original publication. I am grateful to Susan Laity for her erudition and judgment in helping to edit this volume.

My introduction moves back from the ambivalent image of fatherhood in *A Perfect Spy* to meditate upon le Carré's ambivalence toward Kurtz, the leader of the Israeli counterterrorists in *The Little Drummer Girl*. Stefan Kanfer's topical review of *The Honourable Schoolboy* begins the chronological sequence, after which Andrew Rutherford and LeRoy L. Panek, in their different overviews, each contextualize le Carré in the genre of espionage fiction.

In a discussion of three of the major Smiley novels, *Call for the Dead, Tinker, Tailor, Soldier, Spy,* and *Smiley's People,* Abraham Rothberg finds le Carré to be a direct descendent of George Orwell and Aldous Huxley. Holly Beth King on *Tinker, Tailor, Soldier, Spy* and Helen S. Garson on *Call for the Dead* both center upon lively individual achievements of le Carré, while Glenn W. Most finds the author's largest literary context in the two long traditions of the detective novel, American and British. Lars Ole Sauerberg discusses *The Honourable Schoolboy, The Little Drummer Girl,* and *A Small Town in Germany* as instances of England's mediation between America and Germany.

The wit and public man William F. Buckley, Jr., reviews *The Little Drummer Girl* and commends it for being about espionage only as *Madame Bovary* is about adultery. David Monaghan attempts a description of the metaphoric world of le Carré's fiction, which is a kind of wasteland haunted by a quickening entropy.

A Perfect Spy, le Carré's latest and most ambitious novel, is the subject of an acute analysis by Susan Laity, which is published for the first time in this volume. Centering upon the movements of doubling and repetition in the novel, Laity's essay is a powerful defense of le Carré's equivocal relation to the ambivalence of fictive fatherhood in his work, and to his own ambivalence toward his literary fathers, Conrad and Greene. Le Carré's strongest gift, his ear for rendering voices, may also be his greatest flaw, since his own voice remains imitative. Subtly showing how le Carré makes his possible weakness into his strength, Laity's discussion doubtless prophesies a direction that criticism of le Carré will have to take.

Introduction

As the literary son of Graham Greene, John le Carré has no true contemporary rival, unless it be Greene himself. This is the Greene of the "entertainments" from *The Man Within* onwards, including two powerful achievements, *This Gun for Hire* and *Brighton Rock*. Le Carré, it seems to me, resembles Greene more and more, which may not be an altogether good thing, particularly in the recent novels, *The Little Drummer Girl* and *A Perfect Spy*. The image of fatherhood is at best an ambivalent, perhaps even an ambiguous one in *A Perfect Spy*, which begins with a phone call from a man named Jack Brotherhood, calling from London, to a man in Vienna named Magnus Pym. The call is to tell Pym that his father has died, information that Pym welcomes as setting him free. Pym's father, a sublime crook, has shadowed and inhibited his son's life, and in the moment of liberation Pym resolves to write out the story of his own life so as to instruct his own son.

That Pym is a surrogate for le Carré seems clear enough, both in the relation to an actual father and to "the Firm," now called SIS. Axel, Pym's undeserving friend, condemns Pym for a lack of authenticity or originality, as someone put together from bits of other people. Is this le Carré's own anxiety, despite his vast audience and his growing critical acclaim? Are le Carré's novels put together out of Joseph Conrad and Graham Greene, or does he justify Noel Annan's praise? Annan insists that "Le Carré is a natural writer with an unmistakable voice and a vitality that bounces off the page." The vitality can be granted, but the voice sometimes can be mistaken for that of Conrad or Greene. Le Carré's overtly allusive counterpointing of Conrad and Greene against popular spy fiction formulae, from Buchan, Oppenheim, and even Fleming, seems to me a defense against the enormous influence upon him of Conrad's *The Secret Agent* and Greene's spy novels, particularly *The Quiet American* and *Our Man in Havana*.

In *A Perfect Spy*, Pym, a double agent and betrayer of his country, ends as a suicide, once he has concluded his own autobiography, which is addressed to his son:

> Then he hauled the burnbox from the top of the cabinet to the desk and with the two keys from his chain disarmed it and fished out first the files which were too secret to be classified at all and which gave a lot of bogus information about the networks he and Poppy had so painstakingly composed. He chucked them in the waste-paper basket too. When he'd done that he pulled out the gun and loaded it and cocked it, all rather swiftly, and set it on the desk thinking of the many times he had carried a gun and not fired it. He heard a scraping sound from the roof, and said to himself: must be a cat. He shook his head as if to say those damned cats, they get everywhere these days, don't give the birds a chance. He glanced at his gold watch, a wide gesture, remembering that Rick had given it to him and that he might forget to take it off in the bath. So he took it off now and laid it on Tom's envelope and drew a cheerful moon face right next to it, the sign they drew for one another to say "Smile." He undressed and laid his clothes neatly by the bed, then he put on his dressing-gown and took both his towels from the clothes-horse, the big one for the bath, the small one for hands and face. He slipped the gun into the dressing-gown pocket, leaving the safety catch in the "off" position because it was the laborious ethic of the trainers that a safed gun was more dangerous than a live one. He was only going across the corridor but it's a violent world these days and you can't be too careful. About to open the bathroom door he was annoyed to discover that the porcelain knob had stiffened up and scarcely turned. Damned doorknob. Look at that. It took him all the strength of both his hands to twist it and, more annoying still, some idiot must have left soap on it, because his hands kept slithering and he had to use a towel to get a grip. It's probably dear old Lippsie, he thought with a smile: always living in that world inside her head. Placing himself for the last time before the shaving mirror, he arranged the towels around his head and shoulders, making a bonnet of the small one and a cape of the large one, because if there was one thing Miss Dubber hated above another, it was mess. Then he held the gun to where his right ear was, forgetting, as anybody might in the circumstances, whether the trigger of your Browning .38 automatic had two

pressures or just the one. And he noticed how he was leaning: not away from the gun, but into it, like someone a little deaf, straining for a sound.

The best touch here is the last, since Pym has lived his entire life "like someone a little deaf, straining for a sound." If we compare Pym's suicide with Decoud's in Conrad's *Nostromo,* or with the death of Pinkie in Greene's *Brighton Rock,* we are not likely to be much impressed by le Carré's final vision of his most comprehensive and personal hero, surpassing Smiley in pathos and intensity. Conrad's moral complexity is weighted with that great novelist's enigmatic reserve, and is represented by figures as singular as the brilliant Decoud, nihilistic idealist and intellectual man-of-action. Greene's Jacobean sensibility is a poor instrument compared to Conrad's impressionistic apprehension of life's fullness, and yet Greene remains vivid and economical in representation, though never again as memorable as he was in his depiction of Pinkie. Le Carré has lost all sense of economy in *A Perfect Spy*; does he need four hundred and seventy-five pages to render Pym for us? Or would not the book be far more effective at half that length?

Pym, like Decoud and the frightening Pinkie, is a nihilist, and dies a nihilist's death. But Decoud is an authentic and persuasive representation of a nihilistic intellectual, while Pinkie is a damned soul, almost a demon, already in hell while still in this life. Pym is neither a mind nor a soul, however lost. He is essentially a nihilistic child, very much his father's son. Doubtless, this is as le Carré intended it, but can a nihilistic child retain our interest? Le Carré provokes our interest in Pym by suggesting that this perfect spy is truly representative of England today. The contemporary decline of English culture and society is a striking and depressing phenomenon, and is clearly of crucial importance to all of us. *A Perfect Spy* may survive as a social document, as a portrait of England falling outwards and downwards into the abyss of history. Whether so ambitious a novel centered upon a character who lacks the moral courage to enter into the abyss of himself can last as a novel is another question entirely.

II

In his introduction to a book about Kim Philby, le Carré ends by observing that "Philby is the price we pay for being moderately free." The reader is thus reminded that if le Carré is the son of Greene, and grandson of Conrad, he is also a kind of great-nephew to E. M. Forster. Conrad, Greene, and Forster all share in the art of *The Little Drummer Girl,* which seems to me le Carré's best book so far, partly because it lacks the ambitions of *A Perfect Spy* and allows le Carré the distance that Pym cannot afford him. Even Charlie, the English minor actress who is the heroine of *The Little Drummer Girl,* has le Carré's sympathy without the close identification that Pym costs him. The Israelis in the novel, even Kurtz and Joseph, scarcely have le Carré's sympathy, which essentially is with the Palestinians in a very English tradition of choosing sides in that terrible and perpetual war. It is, though, an oddity of *The Little Drummer Girl* that Charlie is a mere stereotype, the Arabs little more, Joseph a failure in representation, while Kurtz is a remarkable success in characterization.

Le Carré's Forsterian moral stance in the novel has little relation to the human realities of the Israeli-Palestinian conflict, and finally becomes quite wearisome. The book's most-quoted sentence is an instance of badly misplaced wit:

> Israeli jets bombed the crowded Palestinian quarter of Beirut, in what was afterwards declared to be an effort to destroy the leadership, though there were no leaders among the several hundred dead—unless of course they were the leaders of tomorrow, for many were children.

This just won't do, since its effect upon me as I reread it now is to make me want to shout at le Carré that there were no leaders among the rabbis and old men massacred by Palestinians last week in an Istanbul synagogue. The problem is not that le Carré takes sides, but rather that a novel had better be unassailable as narrative and characterization if it is to risk such reactions on a reader's part. Le Carré, not being Joseph Conrad, is ill-advised when he takes up such risks.

Yet that is to forget Kurtz, a kind of Israeli Smiley, as several critics have noted. Why Kurtz bears the name of the hero-villain of Conrad's *Heart of Darkness* is a puzzling matter, though not beyond all conjecture. Perhaps because le Carré's Kurtz is also a heroic failure, since he destroys Khalil and his gang and yet cannot thereby help prevent the catastrophic Israeli invasion of Lebanon. Or it may be that Conrad's Kurtz, falling outwards and downwards from enlightenment into darkness, is the forerunner of le Carré's judgment upon his own Kurtz, who in fighting for the light becomes pragmatically indistinguishable from the darkness. Yet le Carré's Kurtz gets away from his creator, and more than Smiley begins to assume a life of his own, a vitality and gusto that transcends le Carré's apparent intentions. For le Carré, Kurtz is the perfect counterterrorist, even as Pym is the perfect spy, and perfect in either case means: to be completely finished in betrayal. But do we read le Carré's Kurtz as being self-betrayed, as Conrad's Kurtz certainly was? Le Carré is equivocal upon this:

> And in the late spring at last, as soon as the Litani basin was dry enough for tanks, Kurtz's worst fears and Gavron's worst threats were fulfilled: the long-awaited Israeli push into Lebanon occurred, ending that present phase of hostilities or, according to where you stood, heralding the next one. The refugee camps that had played host to Charlie were sanitised, which meant roughly that bulldozers were brought in to bury the bodies and complete what the tanks and artillery bombing raids had started; a pitiful trail of refugees set off northward, leaving their hundreds, then their thousands, of dead behind. Special groups eradicated the secret places in Beirut where Charlie had stayed; of the house in Sidon only the chickens and the tangerine orchard remained. The house was destroyed by a team of Sayaret, who also put an end to the two boys Kareem and Yasir. They came in at night, from the sea, exactly as Yasir, the great intelligence officer, had always predicted, and they used a special kind of American explosive bullet, still on the secret list, that has only to touch the body to kill. Of all this—of the effective destruction of her brief love-affair with Palestine—Charlie was wisely spared all knowledge. It could unhinge her, the psychiatrist said; with her imagination and self-absorption, she could perfectly easily hold herself responsible for the entire invasion. Better to keep it from her, therefore; let her find out in her own good time. As to Kurtz, for a month or more he was hardly seen, or, if seen, hardly recognised. His body seemed to shrink to half its size, his Slav eyes lost all their sparkle, he looked his age, whatever that was, at last. Then one day, like a man who has shaken off a long and wasting illness, he returned, and within hours, it seemed, had vigorously resumed his strange running feud with Misha Gavron.

Kurtz, unlike Charlie (and John le Carré), has had no "brief love-affair with Palestine," so that his decline "for a month or more" presumably has to do with his professional ethics, his Smiley-like sense of limits, of a philosophy of restraint, and even of decency, which is after all totally incompatible with counterterrorism. Unlike Smiley, Kurtz is finally a mystery to his creator. Something in Kurtz, a survivor of the Nazi extermination camps, is beyond le Carré's voluntary imagination, and le Carré appears to have the wisdom to know this. Perhaps that is why Kurtz received his Conradian name. It is as though, by such a naming, le Carré both acknowledged his own limits and yet reached out for Conrad's enigmatic magic.

STEFAN KANFER

"Our Impudent Crimes":
The Honourable Schoolboy

In its present emergency, Britain is no longer represented by the Lion and Unicorn. Its new emblem is an owl. His name is George Smiley and he is by all standards a most incongruous symbol. The man is a perpetual cuckold. He is portly, rumpled, bespectacled, with a tendency to puff when ascending stairs and to polish his glasses with his tie. He is donnish and vague. He is also the premier spy of his time.

Which seems fitting. Smiley's creator, John le Carré, 45, is the premier spy novelist of his time. Perhaps of all time. In part, of course, le Carré's success is due to subject matter. Espionage is an immemorial tradition. In Sparta, undercover agents formed the Krypteia—the Secret Force. Two thousand years later the Krypteia remains forceful, but not quite as secret. Scarcely a month passes without some well-broadcast defection from Eastern Europe; hardly a week goes by without some new charge about intelligence excesses in the West. In the post-Watergate epoch, almost any revelation seems credible: accounts of CIA drug experiments and poison cigars, spy satellites and submarine salvage ships, assassination machinations, all more outlandish than any imaginative work. To compete against such headlines, the novelist has to do more than reiterate events; he has to heighten and humanize them. Enter George Smiley.

The spy genre has twin traditions: Great Bad Writing and Great Good Writing. In the Manichaean world of Great Bad Books, evil is always more compelling than heroism. Such works as John Buchan's *The 39 Steps* con-

From *Time*, 3 October 1977. © 1977 by Time, Inc.

struct elaborate international conspiracies; Sax Rohmer's exemplary Fu Man-
chu series features a supervillain "with all the cruel cunning of an entire
Eastern race . . . the Yellow Peril incarnate." From there it is only a bullet's
journey to Ian Fleming's *Doctor No.*

The higher road, paved by Eric Ambler and Graham Greene and im-
proved by le Carré, leads to an ambiguous plane where neither side has a
moral exclusive. The flares of hot and cold wars illuminate enemies with
human faces. The agent's mind is as balkanized as the lands he travels;
betrayal becomes a way of life. The message no longer echoes national an-
thems but T. S. Eliot's *Gerontion*: "Think / Neither fear nor courage saves
us. Unnatural vices / Are fathered by our heroism. Virtues / Are forced upon
us by our impudent crimes."

Those impudent crimes are the subject of le Carré's new volume, *The
Honourable Schoolboy*, published this week in the U.S. Like the author's
dazzling bestsellers, *The Spy Who Came In from the Cold* (1963) and *Tinker,
Tailor, Soldier, Spy* (1974), the latest adventures of Smiley offer the genre a
renewal, not a revolution. "When I first began writing," recalls le Carré,
"Fleming was riding high, and the picture of the spy was that of a character
who could lay the women, and drive the fast car, who used gadgetry and
gimmickry and escape. When I brought back, but did not invent, the realistic
spy story, it was misinterpreted as a great new wave."

The old wave had a tidal force. Le Carré's first books proclaimed a new
talent. *The Spy Who Came In from the Cold* became part of the language.
Its antihero, Alec Leamas, was the personification of that burnt-out case,
that necessary evil, the cold war spy. *Tinker, Tailor* earned more money than
any other espionage novel, and *The Honourable Schoolboy* is about to smash
its record. The novel, now in third printing before publication, is the October
main selection of the Book-of-the-Month Club; paperback rights have been
purchased by Bantam Books for $1 million. The only arena in which *School-
boy* has so far failed to win honors is Hollywood. *Tinker, Tailor* resisted
adaptation; major movie producers judge the new book even harder to film.
One executive recently asked his script department to provide the customary
single-page synopsis, a job as hopeless as carving the Lord's Prayer on the
head of a studio.

For like the ectomorphic Smiley, *The Honourable Schoolboy* resists
shrinkage. Its events are febrile, its local color relentless and sometimes over-
long. This often obscures suspense and the le Carré trademark: a fine irony
that smashes beautiful political theories with hard facts. That irony is apparent in the very word Circus, center of British intelligence. Once a roiling

three-ring operation, the place now resembles a shabby, peeling carnival depleted of funds and dignity.

No one excels le Carré in sense of place—particularly when the place is Secret Service headquarters. The sunless corridors, the peculiar amalgam of research, bureaucratic fatigue and hostility are brilliantly rendered. Power struggles become palpable: Smiley's conversations brim with silences and ambiguities; throwaway lines can hang a man, and one quiet meeting results in a British victory over some brash "cousins" in the CIA. Cruelty abounds, but so does guilt. Smiley believes implicitly in the need for clandestine agents, but he knows that his scholarly gains will soon be absorbed by his dreaded allies—the Americans.

When readers last left Smiley, he had just ferreted out Soviet spy Bill Haydon—a "mole" who for years had unobtrusively buried himself in the British Secret Service. Haydon was manifestly based on Kim Philby, a principal strategist of British intelligence who defected to Russia in 1963 after two decades of spying for the Soviets. Britain's real Secret Service had to be rebuilt after the Philby scandal; the fictional one is equally shattered and in need of repair in the post-Haydon era.

Derided as the "captain of a wrecked ship," Smiley tries to find a coup so stunning it will restore the Circus's reputation—and funding. From the outset, he has one obsessive target: Karla, head of Soviet agent operations, whose spectral face stares down from its frame in Smiley's office. The relationship of the opposing spymasters, playing international chess for men's souls, is worth a book in itself. Karla is an evil genius who once instructed his mole to seduce Smiley's wife—to make the Briton doubt his motives for suspecting Haydon. Smiley's pure, patriotic zeal is simplified, and distorted, by his thirst for revenge.

An opportunity for vengeance occurs one afternoon when attention is drawn to a "gold seam"—a flood of currency—spilling out of Moscow and into Southeast Asia. Is it bankrolling enemy operatives? Is it used to push heroin in the People's Republic of China? Is Drake Ko, an amoral Hong Kong millionaire, a conduit? Drake's brother Nelson is one of the two dozen most important men in Peking and perhaps also a Karla mole, one even more important than Haydon had been. Are the siblings estranged? Or is their relationship thicker than blood? Smiley backtracks through archives and files to find names, places, references once suppressed by Haydon. Midway through the paper chase, coherence emerges. A devious plan unfolds, vouchsafed piecemeal to the anxious reader. The opening moves are made with Jerry Westerby, an aristocratic refugee from occasional Circus assignments now living in the Tuscany hills, where his bookish habits have earned him the sobriquet "the Schoolboy." Westerby carries the spy's classic cards of identity: robust health, womanizing instincts and moral numbness. With words that could have been set to music by Sir Edward Elgar, Smiley reminds his operative of a historian who "wrote of generations that are born into debtors' prisons and spend their lives buying their way to freedom. I think ours is such a generation. Don't you?" Jerry laughs: "Sport, for heaven's sake. You point me and I'll march. Okay?"

The aging adventurer is pointed to Hong Kong, then to Southeast Asia and programmed intrigues—and unexpected sellouts. The Schoolboy's odyssey is both official and personal. As colleagues perish, as the enigmatic Ko brothers become more comprehensible, as loyalties dissolve, Jerry finds himself questioning his own motives and, finally, his orders, the discipline of his "tradecraft." The object of his sudden, intense affection is Drake Ko's beautiful mistress, Lizzie Worthington, an involvement that jeopardizes Westerby's entire mission. The carefully engineered defection of Nelson Ko becomes a ploy within a ploy with apocalyptic result.

Such bare-bones plotting gives only a hint of *The Honourable Schoolboy's* glistening social observation, its luminous intelligence and its immense and varied cast. Among the principals: the incomparable Lizzie, a daydreamy beautiful loser, "punchball" for many lovers, whose flaws prove even more compelling than her easy virtue: "not just the claw marks on her chin, but her lines of travel, and of strain . . . honourable scars from all the battles against her bad luck and her bad judgement." Connie Sachs, Circus Sovietologist beyond compare, "a huge, crippled cunning woman, known to the older hands as Mother Russia." Fawn, Smiley's recessive factotum and "scalp hunter"—professional killer; Craw, an old China hand of archbishoprical speech and mien, shamelessly based on the form and choler of *Sunday Times* Correspondent Richard Hughes: "We colonize them, Your Graces . . . we are hideous not only in their sight, Monsignors, but in their nostrils." Ricardo, the mercenary Mexican pilot: "'How it happened,' he said. 'Listen, I tell you how it happened.' And then I'll kill you, said his eyes." Smaller roles are no less memorable: "My minor characters are always getting out of scale," confesses their creator. "I keep promising them a treat in the next book if they'll just keep quiet now."

He made good that promise with George Smiley, who was a walk-on in *The Spy Who Came In from the Cold*. But these Circus clowns and aerialists will no longer live on promises: in *The Honourable Schoolboy* they jostle and clamor for the reader's attention. Fieldmen, office workers, a parade of journalists and reprobates (*The Honourable Schoolboy* finds the two synonymous), half-castes and Orientals give the book the richness of a Victorian novel of manners.

Le Carré's astringent, melancholy tones will be familiar to anyone who has read his works or those of such eminences as Eric Ambler (*The Mask of Dimitrios*) and Graham Greene (*The Third Man*). Still, Ambler's works are written from the outside with sardonic imagination. Greene's achieve more intimacy, but he is careful to label them as mere "entertainments," like a student caught doodling when he should be cramming for exams. Le Carré carries no such liabilities or self-deprecations. His books are written from the inside out. "There is a kind of fatigue which only fieldmen know" observes *The Honourable Schoolboy*, "a temptation to gentleness which can be the kiss of death." And, "It is a charming arrogance of diplomats the world over to suppose they set an example—to whom, or of what, the devil himself will never know." Such sly *aperçus* are those of Her Majesty's Loyal Opposition, a man who served his term as foreign officer and intelligence operative. As such, le Carré makes no apologies for his work. "The spy form is expanding for me as much as I want," he finds. "I think it's possible to do wonderful things with it."

ANDREW RUTHERFORD

The Spy as Hero:
Le Carré and the Cold War

The ethics of the [spy thriller] genre are far from constant. Espionage in
Kim was still the Great Game which had been played by British officers
throughout much of the nineteenth century to forestall Russian encroach-
ments on India and to establish our hegemony in Central Asia. Sometimes
these agents came to thoroughly unpleasant ends, but the sporting metaphor
they favoured speaks for itself; and the same spirit was often carried over
into fiction. The traditional spy story of the early twentieth century was set
in a world full of hazards but free from moral ambiguities—apart from the
fundamental ambiguity, rarely perceived by the authors or the reading public,
of a double standard applied to espionage and counterespionage activities,
depending on whether these were carried on by "us" or "them." In Buchan's
Richard Hannay stories, the most popular and influential of their kind, the
hero may admire a brave enemy (in the spirit of those who honour while
they cut him down the foe who comes with fearless eyes), but he has a total
confidence, shared by the author, in the rightness of his own cause and the
wrongness of the enemy's. This goes beyond a simple patriotism. Buchan
had an acute sense of the vulnerability of civilised life: "You think," exclaims
the sinister Mr Lumsley in *The Power House* (1913), "that a wall as solid
as the earth separates civilisation from barbarism. I tell you that the division
is a thread, a sheet of glass." This prophetic insight, later praised by Graham
Greene, was accompanied by what has been described (a shade portentously)

From *The Literature of War: Five Studies in Heroic Virtue.* © 1978 by Andrew
Rutherford. Macmillan, 1978.

as Buchan's "Gothic, almost apocalyptic vision of the dark, destructive forces contained in human beings and in society." It is against these, as well as against Germany the nation state, that Hannay is contending; yet he adheres determinedly, quixotically, to decent methods and fair play, whatever devil's work the other side may contemplate. The *locus classicus* occurs in *Mr Standfast* (1919), when Hannay balks at shooting the arch-spy who is planning to destroy the British Army by releasing anthrax germs on its main lines of communication. The discovery of the plot fills him with horror: "I was fairly well used to Boche filthiness, but this seemed too grim a piece of the utterly damnable. I wanted to have Ivery by the throat and force the stuff into his body, and watch him decay slowly into the horror he had contrived for honest men." Yet when "Ivery" appears a few minutes later, Hannay cannot bring himself to act with the appropriate ruthlessness:

> I had my hand on my pistol, as I motioned Mary farther back into the shadows. For a second I was about to shoot. I had a perfect mark and could have put a bullet through his brain with utter certitude. I think if I had been alone I might have fired. Perhaps not. Anyhow now I could not do it. It seemed like potting a sitting rabbit.

It is easy to make fun of such passages, though they stem from an honourable belief that if one must fight, one should fight as cleanly as possible—that if one must touch pitch, one should try to remain undefiled instead of plunging into it and wallowing. The same attitude, which underlies the Geneva Convention itself, survives today in popular fiction and reality, but in a much attenuated form. It has been eroded partly by the sinister appeal of violence in literature and life, but more by the perception that even "clean" fighting necessarily involves considerable ruthlessness. This is even more true of clandestine operations, as the Second World War made manifest.

> To succeed in resistance [writes M. R. D. Foot], you needed extra strong, steely, flexible nerves, no inhibitions at all, and uncanny quickness of wit. As witness . . . "Felix," a Jew of Alsatian-Polish origins who was assistant wireless operator to the young "Alphonse," a British agent in southern France. He, "Alphonse," and "Emanuel" the wireless operator all got out of the same train at Toulouse; "Felix," carrying the transmitter in its readily recognizable suitcase, went up to the barrier first. Two French policemen were conducting a cursory check on identity papers. Behind them, two uniformed SS men were sending everyone with

> a case or big package to the *consigne,* where more SS were making a methodical luggage search. "Felix" took in the scene; ignored the French police; held his suitcase high; and called in authoritative German, "Get me a car at once, I have a captured set." He was driven away in a German-requisitioned car; had it pulled up in a back street; killed the driver, and reported to "Alphonse" with the set for orders.

The situation was pure Buchan; so was Felix's inspired bluff; but the killing of the driver puts the episode in a different moral world.

The secret agents of Cold War fiction move through an even harsher and more brutal world than this; and (unlike Ashenden, in Maugham's pallidly realistic anecdotes of spy-work in the First World War) they are themselves directly involved in its harshness and brutality. The fact that James Bond, their crude prototype, was a professional assassin, licensed officially to kill in cold blood, typifies the moral ambiguity of their proceedings. They share Hannay's sense of being on the side of good against some kind of evil: this is the political and ethical assumption on which their activities and our delight in them are based, though one of the conventions of the genre as it has developed is to allow doubts to arise from time to time in their minds and our own. (There is, for example, a recurrent contrast between the heroic code they live by and the decadence or selfishness of the Western society they are defending.) The main enemy for most of them is not so much communism as Russian tyranny—cruel, oppressive and expansionist, as it revealed itself to be in the postwar years, with its evil nature fully manifested by the methods it employed. Yet their own methods are less scrupulous than Hannay's, and their consciences less tender. They are professionals, not gentleman amateurs, and though they do retain some scruples which help to engage our sympathies, they realise that ruthless enemies have sometimes to be fought by ruthless means. There is therefore a casual tolerance of violence and dirty tricks, so long as they are used in a good cause. "Our kind of work," declares the Master in *The Us or Them War,* "comes with a kind of built-in absolution. All-purpose remission for every imaginable kind of sin on the grounds of higher national interest"; and we relish, with a frisson of delighted horror, the ruthlessness and double-dealing characteristic of the genre. Yet we also go on thinking in terms of good guys versus bad, the inherent contradiction being obscured by the plot-mechanism, which usually allows us to have our moral cake and eat it.

Le Carré offers a more complex pleasure, by combining psychological release with radical moral concern, as distinct from the show of morality which serves in many thrillers as a spice to sin or justification for violence. *The Spy Who Came In from the Cold* (1963) insists upon the inhumanity of actions undertaken nominally on humanity's behalf. Early in the novel, for example, we are brought up sharply by Control's restatement of the fundamental problem of ends and means:

> "The ethic of our work, as I understand it, is based on a single assumption. That is, we are never going to be aggressors. Do you think that's fair?"
>
> Leamas nodded. Anything to avoid talking.
>
> "Thus we do disagreeable things, but we are *defensive*. That, I think, is still fair. We do disagreeable things so that ordinary people here and elsewhere can sleep safely in their beds at night. Is that too romantic? Of course, we occasionally do very wicked things"; he grinned like a schoolboy. "And in weighing up the moralities, we rather go in for dishonest comparisons; after all, you can't compare the ideals of one side with the methods of the other, can you, now?"
>
> Leamas was lost. He'd heard the man talked a lot of drivel before getting the knife in, but he'd never heard anything like this before.
>
> "I mean you've got to compare method with method, and ideal with ideal. I would say that since the war, our methods—ours and those of the opposition—have become much the same. I mean you can't be less ruthless than the opposition simply because your government's *policy* is benevolent, can you now?" He laughed quietly to himself: "That would *never* do," he said.

Control's cynicism and self-satisfaction do not necessarily invalidate his argument, but its more disturbing implications are explored in the action which follows. *The Spy Who Came In from the Cold* combines the excellences of the thriller and the moral fable. It transcends the limitations of the former, but accepts (reluctantly perhaps) those of the latter. The ingenious plot, with its multiple deceptions and double double-crosses, dramatises a cold Machiavellian *real-politik* in which human sympathies have no place. It presents us with a metaphysically bleak world of action, in which for the Christian as much as for the communist the end is seen as justifying the means, and individuals are deliberately sacrificed for the general good. There is a frightening void where one might have expected to find fundamental values: "That is the price they pay," says Leamas of his masters—"to despise God and Karl Marx in the same sentence."

The epigrammatic indictment is a telling one; yet it seems out of character for the uncomprehending Leamas of the earlier dialogue. The thematic
intention is no doubt to show his growing awareness of the issues, but this
is rendered, in the manner of a moral fable, too schematically to be psycho-
logically convincing. On the other hand, the book eschews moral simplicity.
Our Man in Havana stated in a mode of comic fantasy the claims of individual human beings against those of secret services, nation states, or international power blocs. *The Spy Who Came In from the Cold* presents the
same claims as constituents of a tragic dilemma. The sinister power of Russia
and her satellites, and their threat to "ordinary people here and elsewhere"
are self-evident within the novel. Kipling's Wall was an impressive barrier
against Rome's enemies, for the protection of her citizens and subjects. The
Wall against which Leamas and Liz are shot is a barrier to prevent East
Germany's own citizens from escaping to the West, and it is described sig-
nificantly as "a dirty, ugly thing of breeze blocks and strands of barbed wire,
lit with cheap yellow light, like the backdrop for a concentration camp."
The need for secret services as one line of defence in such a world is real—
not illusory as it was shown to be in Greene's Havana. Leamas, even in his
revulsion from his calling, sees it as necessary "for the safety of ordinary,
crummy people like you and me," and the fact that it condemns them both
to death does not dispose of his contention. Certainly the final note is one
of protest. Leamas himself turns out to be a pawn in the game in which we
thought he was a knight; and Liz, for all her half-baked communism, is an
innocent victim whose death evokes the image of a child in a small car
smashed between great lorries. The pathos of the end is modified only by
Leamas's own final act of affirmation. His climbing down the Wall to die
with her instead of jumping to safety, his refusal to go on living on the terms
he would be left with, is in its way a triumph of the spirit. Yet the dilemma
the book poses remains unresolved. As in *Kim,* where the claims of contemplation are weighed against those of action—the world of the Lama against
that of Mahbub Ali—our satisfaction comes not from being presented with
a neat solution, but from seeing the incompatible alternatives so powerfully
presented.

We are left with the question whether it is possible to be a secret agent
and a fully human being—or rather, since the agent in this formula is merely
an exemplar, whether personal integrity can ever be preserved in the cor-
rupting world of action. The true le Carré hero, Smiley, is the test case. He
had already figured as protagonist in *Call for the Dead* (1961) and *A Murder
of Quality* (1962). Neither book aspired to be more than a good thriller,
but they established him as a more fully apprehended character than Lea-

mas—an unfashionable secret agent fully aware of the psychological and moral hazards of his calling.

> His emotions in performing this work [of selecting German agents before the war] were mixed, and irreconcilable. It intrigued him to evaluate from a detached position what he had learnt to describe as "the agent potential" of a human being; to devise minuscule tests of character and behaviour which could inform him of the qualities of a candidate. This part of him was bloodless and inhuman—Smiley in this role was the international mercenary of his trade, amoral and without motive beyond that of personal gratification.
>
> Conversely it saddened him to witness in himself the gradual death of natural pleasure. Always withdrawn, he now found himself shrinking from the temptations of friendship and human loyalty; he guarded himself warily from spontaneous reaction. By the strength of his intellect, he forced himself to observe humanity with clinical objectivity, and because he was neither immortal nor infallible he hated and feared the falseness of his life.

Against this, however, worked his love of England, his hatred of Nazism, which constituted for him a clear unambiguous enemy, and his capacity for sympathy and pity, which was to grow from his own suffering. He had been recruited at Oxford by his tutor Jebedee, now dead. ("He had boarded a train at Lille in 1941 with his radio operator, a young Belgian, and neither of them had been heard of again.") Smiley's own exploits were of that wartime past, viewed now with middle-aged, elegiac regret. In spite of, or perhaps because of, his sensitivity, he had done well. ("'The best,' Adrian had said. 'The strongest and the best.'") But there is a frank acknowledgement of the nervous strain he had had to endure, and the toll it took of him:

> He had never guessed it was possible to be frightened for so long. He developed a nervous irritation in his left eye which remained with him fifteen years later; the strain etched lines on his fleshy cheeks and brow. He learnt what it was never to sleep, never to relax, to feel at any time of day or night the restless beating of his own heart, to know the extremes of solitude and self-pity, the sudden unreasoning desire for a woman, for drink, for exercise, for any drug to take away the tension of his life.

This sketches in his past: his present is one of apparent mediocrity and failure, disproved only in action. Unimpressive in appearance, scholarly by temperament, middle-aged and middle-class, cuckolded by his aristocratic wife, a figure of some pathos though also of hidden strength, Smiley is portrayed in greater depth than either of these narratives really requires. He seems a character in search of a plot which will be adequate, as these are not, to his potential.

He reappears in *The Spy Who Came In from the Cold* in a minor but ambiguous role. (Each of le Carré's works is self-contained and self-sufficient, but cumulatively they reinforce each other, as the same characters or themes recur in different contexts.) We gather that he was opposed to the whole operation, but once it is launched he takes an active part, providing the incriminating evidence to be seized on by the East German tribunal. Near the very end, however, we glimpse his concern for the two victims:

> [Leamas] heard a voice in English from the Western side of the wall:
> "Jump, Alec! Jump man!"
> Now everyone was shouting, English, French and German, mixed; he heard Smiley's voice from quite close:
> "The girl, where's the girl?"

He figures comparably in *The Looking Glass War* (1965), that study in futility, self-deception and betrayal. The mission which we follow with ex-cited apprehension is misconceived and badly executed, but it is also delib-erately aborted by Control to discredit finally the remnant of the rival service which had mounted it. Smiley, high now in the counsels of the Circus, in-dicates revulsion when he realises what Control has done, what he himself has been involved in, though it falls to him to close the operation down, leaving the agent to his fate. As well as dissecting the ruthlessness of inter-service rivalries, the novel exposes a corrupt nostalgia for wartime experi-ence, and the desire this breeds in the young as well as in the middle-aged to relive or replay a supposedly heroic past; but from this spiritual temp-tation Smiley seems immune. In contrast with the febrile enthusiasm, the pathetic aspirations of Leclerc's organisation, he figures, in the glimpses which we have of him, as highly professional, enigmatic, yet humane.

In both these novels he is more a function than a character; in *Tinker, Tailor, Soldier, Spy* (1974) he holds the centre of the stage. Le Carré here allows himself the amplitude and the complexity of treatment of the novel proper, though his conventions remain those of the spy thriller. These are in no way disabling. Greene had already proved their value in his entertainments and more serious fiction as images or paradigms of normal experience. And in le Carré's *A Small Town in Germany* (1968), a considerable novel in its own right, the security investigation had revealed not the suspected flight of a defector, but a tangled web of professional and personal relationships, of loyalties and betrayals, in the British Embassy at Bonn. The investigating agent there became the novelist's device for uncovering the truths of character and ultimate belief concealed by the facade which constitutes daily reality. A similar device is now employed in Smiley's struggle to identify a traitor high in the security service itself. As he threads his way through the labyrinth of evidence, each character whom he encounters, each interview that he con-ducts, helps to throw light on the central problem of disloyalty, but also provides insights into a wide spectrum of personalities and values. It is through the process of investigation that the novel creates its own fully authenticated human world. The main structural motif of a quest, difficult and perilous in the extreme, culminating in a confrontation with the powers of evil—a quest undertaken by a solitary hero with (in this case) a few trusted followers—gives unity and tension to the narrative. (*The Naive and Senti-mental Lover,* the one work in which le Carré totally rejects the thriller framework, is curiously flabby by comparison.) We relish, as we do in works by Adam Hall, Len Deighton, William Haggard, all the technicalities of secret service work—the arcane tradecraft: realism of presentation is common form in the spy thriller, even when the content is plainly fantasy. The extent to which le Carré's realism extends here to content could, however, be a matter for debate. Kim Philby complained of *The Spy Who Came In from the Cold* that "the whole plot, from beginning to end, is basically implausible—at any rate to anyone who has any real knowledge of the business"; but few of us can claim such knowledge, and Philby's own career outdid spy fiction in its bizarre actuality, forcing us to reconsider our criteria of probability. Perhaps it will suffice that *Tinker, Tailor, Soldier, Spy* carries enough conviction for us to suspend our lingering disbelief; and its significance, in any case, is not confined to the esoteric world of secret agents which provides its subject matter: it is to be read analogically as well as literally.

This novel is not primarily concerned with ends and means, though that theme was to be restated in *The Honourable Schoolboy* (1977), in which Smiley broods on the paradox of being "*inhuman in defence of our humanity, . . . harsh in defence of compassion; . . . single-minded in defence of our disparity.*" The concern here is intense but oddly intermittent, failing to inform the narrative as a whole: the over-researched plot of *The Honourable Schoolboy* is expanded and elaborated to a point where it begins to disap-point us structurally and thematically. Whereas *Tinker, Tailor, Soldier, Spy* achieves a perfect fusion of spy plot and universal theme, as it explores the antithetical phenomena of treason and fidelity.

The world it presents us with is one of multiple betrayals—of treason, infidelity, disloyalty and broken faith. Bill Roach, the pathetically vulnerable schoolboy of the sub-plot, suffers from his parents' broken marriage. His case is juxtaposed with the absurd one of the headmaster's father, who has run away with a receptionist from the nearby hotel, gladly abandoning wife, son and school. That two former teachers have been guilty of breaches of trust and of the law, is a comic-satiric detail reinforcing the main theme. The unfaithfulness of Smiley's wife, especially her liaison with Bill Haydon, is a motif which recurs in conversation after conversation, as well as in Smiley's own tortured awareness. Sexual infidelity is paralleled by professional disloyalty. Networks are blown, operations aborted and agents liquidated, by covert treachery. Irina, offering to defect to Britain with key information about the traitor, is herself betrayed and shipped back to Moscow (as the wretched Volkov was by Philby's own manipulations). Above all, Jim Prideaux, simple, kindly, patriotic, now part-crippled by his wound, was shot in the back, literally and metaphorically, on a mission which turned out to be a baited trap. Examples of treachery, of obligations broken and trust betrayed, proliferate like the metaphorical extensions of sin and disorder in Shakespearean tragedy. There is a sense of corruption at the very heart of things; and Smiley's search for the source of evil has affinities with Oedipus's quest for truth or Hamlet's for revenge.

The tension of the plot depends on all—or almost all—foreknowledge of the outcome being withheld. We work through the evidence with Smiley himself, and it is only in retrospect or on rereading, when our knowledge is complete, that we realise how closely textured the whole narrative has been— how devoid of superfluities, and how potently functional in its elaborated detail. In the opening chapter, for example, the dialogue between Bill Roach and Jim seems so simply naturalistic that we do not on first reading give its trivialities a second thought:

> "New boy, eh? Well *I'm* not a new boy," Jim went on, in altogether a much more friendly tone. . . . "I'm an old boy. Old as Rip Van Winkle if you want to know. Older. Got any friends?"
>
> "No sir," said Roach simply, in the listless tone which schoolboys always use for saying "no," leaving all positive response to their interrogators. Jim however made no response at all, so that Roach felt an odd stirring of kinship suddenly, and of hope.
>
> "My other name's Bill," he said. "I was christened Bill but Mr Thursgood calls me William."
>
> "Bill, eh. The unpaid Bill. Anyone ever call you that?"

"No, sir."

"Good name, anyway."

"Yes, sir."

"Known a lot of Bills. They've all been good 'uns."

We soon realise, however, that Jim *is* a Rip Van Winkle in still holding to a simple, old-fashioned patriotism. By the end we know that he has said "no" repeatedly to interrogators worse than any Bill Roach has encountered. We also know by then that he was deliberately betrayed to captivity and torture, if not death, by his oldest, closest friend, Bill Haydon—one Bill who was not a good 'un. And the unpaid Bill of the opening is settled well and truly when Jim, following in Smiley's footsteps, comes on his betrayer and leaves him with his neck as neatly broken as that of the owl he had disposed of when it fluttered down the classroom chimney. "Only a gamekeeper, declared Sudely, who had one, would know how to kill an owl so well"; and we recognise Jim's handiwork when we read, some three hundred pages later, that "[Haydon's] eyes were open and his head was propped unnaturally to one side, like the head of a bird when its neck has been expertly broken."

It would be hypocritical to deny that while we relish the plot parallels and verbal echoes (Freud's forepleasures), we feel deeper satisfaction at this even-handed justice, meted out by the man who has suffered most from Haydon's treachery. The revenge ethic seems appropriate in circumstances such as these; moral revulsion is not invoked as a response; but we are left to speculate on the degree of perturbation in Jim's spirit.

> For the rest of that term, Jim Prideaux behaved in the eyes of Roach much as his mother had behaved when his father went away. He spent a lot of time on little things, like fixing up the lighting for the school play and mending the soccer nets with string, and in French he took enormous pains over small inaccuracies. But big things, like his walks and solitary golf, these he gave up altogether, and in the evenings stayed in and kept clear of the village. Worst of all was his staring, empty look when Roach caught him unawares, and the way he forgot things in class, even red marks for merit: Roach had to remind him to hand them in each week.

Roach's perceptions are sound even though his understanding is inadequate—Jim had praised him, we remember, as a watcher—and his opening comparison is apter than he knows. The emotion Jim conceals, or reveals intermittently, while he is lying low after the murder, is presumably not guilt but grief, at having been betrayed by someone he had loved.

The nature of Bill Haydon's treason is defined indeed largely in terms of its personal implications. "[He] had betrayed," Smiley reflects. "As a lover, a colleague, a friend; as a patriot; as a member of that inestimable body which Ann loosely called the Set: in every capacity, Haydon had overtly pursued one aim and secretly achieved its opposite. Smiley knew very well that even now he did not grasp the scope of that appalling duplicity. . . ." This scope, however, is precisely what the novel reveals to us. The excuses and explanations which are offered cannot reconcile us to the facts—Haydon's making love to Ann only to cloud Smiley's judgement; his sacrificing Jim—his old comrade-in-arms in more senses than one—only to discredit Control and safeguard his own secret; his systematic betrayal of all the colleagues and subordinates who had trusted and admired him. "I hate the idea of causes," E. M. Forster wrote in 1939, "and if I had to choose between betraying my country and betraying my friend, I hope I should have the guts to betray my country." The forcible-feeble challenge assumes an ethic based exclusively on personal relationships, ignoring the truth George Eliot insists on, that "there is no private life which has not been determined by a wider public life." Forster does not pause to consider whether the betrayal of his country (*anno domini* 1939) might involve the betrayal of not one but many friends, and the violation of personal relationships on a nightmare scale. Yet the opposite extreme of an ethic based exclusively on public life, with its impersonal abstractions like patriotism or communism, is equally illusory. Man, as the realistic novel continually reminds us, is uniquely individual but also, and essentially, a social animal, existing by his very nature in a complex of relationships with, and obligations to, his fellow-men and women; and any moral judgement on his actions must take due account of these.

Romance does frequently detach its heroes from this social context, so as to deal (as James puts it) with "experience liberated . . . experience disengaged, disembroiled, disencumbered, exempt from the conditions that we usually know to attach to it." It therefore lends itself to great symbolic actions—quests and conflicts, for example, which tend to the allegorical— but romance achieves its greatest intensity, James argues, "when the sacrifice of community, of the 'related' sides of situations, has not been too rash." Too rash it may well be in most spy thrillers, delighting as they do in solitary heroes untrammelled by normal social ties and obligations. (Even when they are members of an organisation, they often rebel against the bureaucrats who run it; they usually disregard it when it interferes with their activities; and they are in any case on their own when facing greatest danger: this, of course, is part of their imaginative appeal.) In *Tinker, Tailor, Soldier, Spy* le Carré reestablishes the human context, the sense of community and the "related" sides of situations in his espionage plot. To understand Haydon's betrayal of his country is to see that it involves the betrayal of his class, his profession, his own past—but also of his colleagues, friends and intimates. Jim Prideaux's role is a symbolic one, although his story is moving and horrifying in its own right. The analysis is moral rather than ideological or sociological as it was in le Carré's earlier comments on the Philby case. Haydon is shown to have a basic cynicism, a calloused sensibility of the kind Philby unwittingly reveals in his own memoirs. Betrayal has become for him a habit, a lifestyle, which he extends even to old friends, or present intimates like the girl with the baby (his, presumably) in the squalid flat in Kentish Town, whom he pays off with a cheque for £1,000 as he prepares to leave for Moscow.

Smiley, on the other hand, is a man of feeling, with an overwhelming, almost an exaggerated sense of responsibility (glimpsed in his distress when Lacon's daughter tumbles from her pony). Instead of seeking personal revenge on Haydon, he argues for trading him to Russia in exchange for the agents behind the Iron Curtain whose identities have been betrayed. We last see him humbly bound for an attempted reconciliation with his wife. He shows a sensitive awareness of the personalities, the prejudices, the susceptibilities, of the people whom he has to deal with, and he is throughout a man of conscience. In all respects but courage and professional skill he is the antithesis of Haydon, who had been a more glamorous figure, but whose heroism had had no firm moral basis. Even at his romantic best, as a "latter day Lawrence of Arabia," Haydon had embodied Conrad's "spirit of adventure" rather than the "spirit of service" of which Smiley is a representative.

> The mere love of adventure is no saving grace [Conrad wrote in *Notes on Life and Letters*]. It is no grace at all. It lays a man under no obligation of faithfulness to an idea and even to his own self. Roughly speaking, an adventurer may be expected to have courage, or at any rate may be said to need it. But . . . there is no sort of loyalty to bind him in honour to consistent conduct.

This was indeed what Haydon lacked, though he had been an inspiration to younger men like Peter Guillam, to whom he had seemed "the torch-bearer of a certain kind of antiquated romanticism, a notion of English calling which—for the very reason that it was vague and understated and elusive— had made sense of Guillam's life till now." This ideal is now tarnished by treachery, as are "the plain, heroic standards [Guillam] wished to live by";

and we have the sense of reaching the end of an era when the traditional, upper-class, clubland hero is unmasked as a villain. There remains, however, the alternative of Smiley himself—unromantic, humdrum, but dependable. His ultimate beliefs remain uncertain, as do Haydon's. He is capable, at the moment he establishes Bill's guilt, of "a surge of resentment against the institutions he was supposed to be protecting"; and once, when his guard is down, he reveals a basic scepticism about the moral-political claims of East and West. But we know him, as we know Bill Haydon, by his works. He lives in practice by a code of loyalty, of fidelity, of obligation—to his wife, his subordinates, his colleagues, his profession, ultimately his country; and the human value of this ethic is established fictionally, proved on our pulses, by the action of the novel. Its polarities tend ultimately to the allegorical: Smiley and Haydon are fully rendered, fully individualised characters, but in the roles of agent and double agent, hero and villain, they emerge as representatives of integrity and corruption in a world of crumbling values, which can be sustained, it seems, only by bleak courage and loyalty without much faith.

Yet the novel itself implies a faith—not so much in a country or political system (though le Carré's preference is clear), as in man himself—in his capacity to live humbly, yet heroically and sacrificially, a life of service. ("The modern world," observes Ralph Harper, "has thought up many ways to diminish man, and the thriller is one way we have to affirm our belief in a human nature that, while menaced on all sides, has not withered beyond recognition and admiration.") It is true that Smiley's triumph is precarious, and the sequel to this novel is to end with his defeat. The power politics of Whitehall will soon relegate him to retirement, and reduce him to despair; his aides will once more be demoted; the CIA will reap the benefit of his last great coup; and Ann will go on being unfaithful. All he has achieved is to stave off one specific danger—to keep the whole system running till another crisis supervenes; but perhaps that is the most that anyone can do. "There *is* no product," Bradfield exclaims near the end of *A Small Town in Germany*: "There *is* no final day. This *is* the life we work for. Now. At this moment. Every night, as I go to sleep, I say to myself: another day achieved. Another day added to the unnatural life of a world on its death-bed. And if I never relax; if I never lift my eye, we may run on for another hundred years." The soldier's and the secret agent's work is more spectacular than his, but their claims would not be greater.

LeROY L. PANEK

Espionage Fiction
and the Human Condition

David John Moore Cornwell chose a pen name without regard for people who have to write it as a possessive. The name le Carré, though, does bring to mind a number of important associations. It echoes the name of one of the inventors of the spy novel, William le Queux, and it demonstrates the tensions so important to Cornwell's own spy novels. With its French meaning, the square, le Carré stands for the finished geometrical figure opposed to le Queux, the line, limping along to infinity. The figure of the square also represents the antithesis to the circle, the Circus, the name of the spy organization which le Carré invents and chronicles in his novels. To date, Cornwell has used the name le Carré for seven espionage books: *Call for the Dead* (1961), *The Spy Who Came In from the Cold* (1963), *The Looking Glass War* (1965), *A Small Town in Germany* (1968), and the Karla trilogy— *Tinker, Tailor, Soldier, Spy* (1974), *The Honourable Schoolboy* (1977), and *Smiley's People* (1980). Le Carré is also the pseudonym for Cornwell's two non-espionage novels, *A Murder of Quality* (1962), a detective novel featuring George Smiley, and *The Naive and Sentimental Lover* (1971), a regular novel contrasting the worlds of the bourgeois and the artist.

Le Carré connects himself with the established traditions of the English spy novel. He does this through the associations of the pseudonym of le Carré, and he also acknowledges John Buchan in choosing Mr. Standfast for his hero's workname, and in borrowing the name of Craw in *The Honourable*

From *The Special Branch: The British Spy Novel, 1890–1980*. © 1981 by Bowling Green University Popular Press.

Schoolboy from Buchan's newspaper proprietor in *Castle Gay* (1930). Nevertheless, le Carré represents those things which are most contemporary in the spy novel. Unlike the fantasies of Fleming or Hall, le Carré portrays an enervated Britain reeling from its fall from international power and its own internal problems. He uses the spy organization to examine not necessarily spies, but the way in which men serve institutions and institutions serve men. Chiefly, though, he uses the spy novel as a vehicle to explore human identity and the actions and reactions which contribute meaning to otherwise empty lives. Finally, le Carré has concentrated upon the literary craftsmanship of the spy book. None of his fictions comes out overnight following the same pat literary formula. His first novel, *Call for the Dead,* shows all of the tightness and consciousness of a first-class literary maker, and he has continued to develop his skills in the complex point of view and the intricate plots of his recent novels. In his most recent novels, *The Honourable School-boy* and *Smiley's People,* le Carré tends to turn inward and backward, developing the past of his own fictional world. Rather than narcissism, though, this represents a general trend in literature, from Updike's *Rabbit Redux* to Barth's *Letters,* to return and augment early material, to contrast the past with the present, or to acknowledge the creation of a world and its people as the most important facet of literary imagination. All of these elements move le Carré out of the category of popular fiction into the class of regular literature. With *The Honourable Schoolboy,* particularly, average readers begin reading with the notion that they will enjoy this best-seller; they proceed with the idea that they ought to appreciate the novel which reviewers have praised, but they then give it up whining that it is too confusing, too hard. This is, of course, absurd: try Pynchon, try Barth, try Burgess. Le Carré does not really challenge us as readers. If he is difficult, it is because his world and ours is difficult; his manner of presentation is not simply that of beginning, middle, and end, but then real stories do not develop simply. After Conrad, le Carré gives us the most thorough, the most realistic, the most thoughtful, and therefore the most disturbing, portrait of the secret world found in spy fiction.

Le Carré began writing about spies because of the security crisis in postwar Britain. Literally, George Smiley, the principal spy in the le Carré novels, enters, or reenters, the secret world in the first novel instead of staying at Oxford because of "the revelations of a young Russian cypher-clerk in Ottawa [who] had created a new demand for men of Smiley's experience." This refers to the actual defection of Igor Gouzenko on September 5, 1945; Gouzenko's defection led to the falling dominoes of arrests, trials, and defections in the fifties: the arrests of Alan Nunn May and Klaus Fuchs for passing on nuclear secrets, and the defections of Bruno Pontecorvo, Guy Burgess, Donald Maclean, and, finally, Kim Philby. In *Call for the Dead*, le Carré twice alludes to Maclean and Fuchs (he avoids mentioning Burgess, perhaps because of his insignificance as a security danger or perhaps because of the complexities raised by the fact that both Burgess and le Carré were old Eton boys—although in *The Naive and Sentimental Lover,* the heroes adopt the pseudonyms of Burgess and Maclean for a night on the town in Paris). Throughout most of his books le Carré centers his plots on double agents, moles, and defections. *Call for the Dead* concerns the security clearance of Fennan, a Foreign Office official controlled by the East Germans. *The Spy Who Came In from the Cold* reverses things and deals with a British agent in the woodwork of East German security. *Tinker, Tailor* is a Philby novel, tracing the discovery of a Soviet mole in the garden of British security. A Soviet mole in the People's Republic of China lies at the heart of *The Honourable Schoolboy. Smiley's People* concludes a motif begun in *Tinker, Tailor,* showing the successful intimidation of a Soviet official in order to force him to defect. The double agent opens up all sorts of fictional possibilities for the spy writer. Le Carré could have treated this material on a simple game level (you hide them, we find them), or he could have played it as an international game (Soviets 4; British 4), but he does not. Double agents and defectors are more than plot material. Le Carré views defection in somewhat the same light as Greene does in *The Human Factor*: it is a test of consciousness, not so much for the individual who leaves, mentally or physically, but for those who remain behind and must deal with themselves.

For le Carré man is essentially an isolated, undefined entity, existing in a world which is terribly difficult but one in which identity is possible on a number of levels. To find the essential le Carré, we need first to consider the phrases which he repeats in one novel after another. The first is a quotation from Hesse, here taken from *Call for the Dead*:

> But who could tell? What did Hesse write? "Strange to wander in the mist, each is alone." We know nothing of one another, nothing. Smiley mused. However closely we live together, at whatever time of day or night we sound the deepest thoughts in one another, we know nothing.

Like this statement on human isolation, le Carré repeats in several novels an anecdote illustrating the emptiness of existence. Here Smiley recites it to a murder suspect in *A Murder of Quality*:

> "You know, Fielding," he said at last, "we just don't know

what people are like, we can never tell; there isn't any truth about human beings, no formula that meets each one of us. And there are some of us—aren't there?—who are nothing, who are so labile that we astound ourselves; we're the chameleons. I read a story once about a poet who bathed himself in cold fountains so that he could recognize his own existence in the contrast. He had to reassure himself, you see, like a child being hateful to its parents. You might say he had to make the sun shine on him so that he could see his shadow and feel alive."

If bathing in fountains is an effete method of demonstrating one's existence, le Carré introduces a sterner, more authoritative passage in several of the novels. Here, Jerry Westerby solves his crisis of motivation by recalling it and later acting upon it:

Even now, he needed that long to bring himself to the point, because Jerry at heart was a soldier and voted with his feet. *In the beginning was the deed,* Smiley liked to say to him, in his failed-priest mood, quoting from Goethe. For Jerry that simple statement had become a pillar of his uncomplicated philosophy. What a man thinks is his own business. What matters is what he does. [le Carré's italics]

This is a definitive statement for the heroes in le Carré, but he uses other motifs to shape the hero's consciousness. First comes a point about the proper shaping of doubt. This runs through *The Looking Glass War,* but Alan Turner in *A Small Town in Germany* gives it its fullest formulation:

He looked once more at the diary and thought: Question fundamentals. Madam, show this tired schoolboy your fundamentals, learn the parts, read the book from scratch—that was your tutor's advice, and who are you to ignore the advice of your tutor? Do not ask *why* Christ was born on Christmas Day—ask whether he was born at all.

Even if one knows the proper question, people in le Carré face situations in which all solutions are equally true or equally false. To establish this situation in his books, from the last chapter in *Call for the Dead* ("Between Two Worlds") to *Smiley's People,* le Carré implies these lines from Arnold's "Stanzas from the Grand Chartreuse":

Wandering between two worlds, one dead
The other powerless to be born

With nowhere yet to rest my head,
Like these, on earth, I wait forlorn.

People do not, though, have to moulder among monkish crypts for le Carré has another alternative, again contained in a quotation, which he occasionally brings in. In *Tinker, Tailor* Roy Bland gives us this solution: "An artist is a bloke who can hold two fundamentally opposing views and still function." So says F. Scott Fitzgerald and so says le Carré. The formula, then, goes: isolation, questioning, knowledge of relativity, synthesis, action. Out of these literary fragments le Carré builds a path of behavior, a body of characters, nine plots, and his world.

Le Carré bases his world on the fact, stated by Hesse, that we know very little about other people. Just as importantly, his characters know very little about themselves. In the novels le Carré puts his people into circumstances in which they have opportunities to find out about themselves or, failing this, to absorb identity from their surroundings. On the easiest level, the institution—whether the Department of *The Looking Glass War* or the Circus—provides roles, goals, and identities for its employees. We can see this with characters like Connie Sachs, "Mother Russia," in the Karla trilogy. In spite of her eccentricities, without her archives and the direction given by research, Connie, as seen in *Smiley's People,* is a gin-sodden wreck, facing the horror of death without props or resources. The Circus, too, gives focus to the lives of bureaucrats and wheeler-dealers in le Carré. Saul Enderby and Sam Collins act as chameleons in *The Honourable Schoolboy* and *Smiley's People,* coloring themselves to fit the current requisites of their jobs or the temporary hue of international affairs. Thus Collins, in the first book, is a sinister figure clawing his way up to a permanent job on the fifth floor, but, having achieved this, in *Smiley's People,* he becomes a grinning, brow-beaten toady because his situation demands it. All of this culminates in *The Looking Glass War,* where le Carré presents a full-scale demonstration of institutions making people's lives. Here Taylor, Avery, Leclerc, Haldane, Leiser, and even the janitors draw their moods, their very beings from the Department. Thus le Carré opens up Avery's mind and shows that:

> He thanked Leclerc, thanked him warmly, for the privilege of knowing these men, for the excitement of this mission; for the opportunity to advance from the uncertainty of the past toward experience and maturity, to become a man shoulder to shoulder with the others, tempered in the fire of war; he thanked him for the precision of command, which made order out of the anarchy of his heart.

For all of the agents in the field, Leamas, Leiser, Westerby, the institution provides a prepackaged identity not only with the false papers and cover story, but, more importantly, in the prescribed rules of behavior drummed into them at training school and in the goal of the mission itself. Therefore, at the end of *The Spy Who Came In from the Cold,* when Leamas has lost his illusions about almost everything else, he still believes in his mission:

> "There's only one law in this game," Leamas retorted. "Mundt is their man; he gives them what they need. That's easy enough to understand, isn't it? Leninism—the expediency of temporary alliances. What do you think spies are: priests, saints and martyrs? They're a squalid procession of vain fools, traitors, too, yes; pansies, sadists, and drunkards, people who play cowboys and Indians to brighten their rotten lives. Do you think they sit like monks in London, balancing rights and wrongs? I'd have killed Mundt if I could, I hate his guts; but not now. It so happens that they need him. They need him so that the great moronic mass you admire can sleep soundly in their beds at night. They need him for the safety of ordinary, crummy people like you and me."

If we know nothing of ourselves, le Carré says, spying and its institutions can give us identities—identities which can be base or which can be noble.

The problem with this sort of identity resides in the fact that "there isn't any formula that meets each one of us." The agent is a human being and consequently imponderable. In *The Looking Glass War,* Haldane, the old spy, answers Avery's query about agents' motives only with questions: "Why do agents ever do anything? Why do any of us. . . . Why do they consent or refuse, why do they lie or tell the truth? Why do any of us?" During the course of each of the le Carré novels, the hero steps out of line, breaks the pattern, sees other goals and identities and commits himself to them. In *The Spy Who Came In from the Cold,* Leamas commits himself to love; Leiser, in *The Looking Glass War,* on a lesser scale, does the same thing; Leo, in *A Small Town in Germany,* commits himself to justice; Jerry, in *The Honourable Schoolboy,* commits himself to love; and George Smiley does a similar thing by refusing the victor's spoils at the close of *Call for the Dead, Tinker, Tailor, The Honourable Schoolboy,* and *Smiley's People.* These acts define these particular characters; these are the plunges into cold fountains; these are the proofs, not of December 25, but of Christ's existence. Fixing identity, committing oneself, in *The Spy Who Came In from the Cold, The Looking Glass War, A Small Town in Germany,* and *The Honourable Schoolboy,* comes only with the hero's death. Only then can his identity remain fixed and stable in a world whose only constant is change.

On a personal level, le Carré gives his characters worlds in which little remains stable: wives betray husbands, husbands destroy wives, friends betray friends, students reject teachers, individuals deceive themselves. Smiley's marriage, Avery's marriage, Lacon's marriage, Lizzie Worthington's marriage, even Karla's [common-law] marriage all split apart, leaving characters between love and isolation, commitment and isolation. The world in le Carré is not, however, chaotic: from the very first novel, le Carré builds his fictional world on polar issues, and he continues to portray a world of opposites in each novel. The mind versus the body, the past versus the present, contemplation versus action, secrecy versus intimacy, the institution versus the individual, aloofness versus consciousness, the Cousins (the CIA) versus the Circus, the state versus the individual, absolutism versus relativity: these are some of the alternatives upon which le Carré strings his novels. A certain type of person (for le Carré, the bureaucrat) thrives in this world of ambiguities, like an amphibian living on both land and water but never wedded to either. For his heroes, however, it is an unbearable strain to live an uncommitted, undefined existence. They cannot tolerate the position of being "between two worlds," and they act, they engage themselves to one of the alternatives and pass out of the world of flux. They all do it except George Smiley, the continuing hero of the le Carré novels, who, like Fitzgerald's artist, repeatedly attempts to find a human path between clashing extremes.

Le Carré brings George Smiley into all of his spy novels except *A Small Town in Germany*, which is an experiment with the hard-boiled hero. In *The Spy Who Came In from the Cold* and *The Looking Glass War* Smiley plays minor roles, but even in these books his appearance is important to the message of the plot. In fact, the author's desire to include his continuing character in his plots causes le Carré to make Smiley a menacing character in *The Spy Who Came In from the Cold* because he wants to include Smiley but cannot invent a role for his humanistic nature in this plot. Despite this one breach of artistic judgment, le Carré has spent a good deal of his creative energy since 1961 in delineating Smiley and comparing other characters to him in order to make points about the human condition.

Physically, George Smiley is a made-to-measure antihero. He is, in the term which le Carré applies to several other characters, "one of life's losers." In the context of the schoolboy novel, Smiley would be the nonathletic fat boy. In the context of the adult espionage novel, he remains the fat boy, the outsider. At the beginning of *Call for the Dead*, le Carré introduces him to us: "Short, fat, and of a quiet disposition, he appeared to spend a lot of money on really bad clothes, which hung about his squat frame like skin on a shrunken toad." Especially in the early novels le Carré keeps the image of the toad attached to Smiley: his wife, in remembered conversations, calls him "toad" and "toad lover." Le Carré makes Smiley a largely passive character. He wants to be left alone, and other people (Frey, Control, Haydon, Karla) initiate the action in the novels while another group of characters (Mendel, Prideaux, Westerby, Guillam, Fawn, Toby) performs the important deeds in the books. As we can see in *A Murder of Quality*, Smiley comes from the tradition of the cerebral detective and not from the tradition of the spy hero. Especially in *Call for the Dead* le Carré emphasizes not his physical acts but Smiley's intellectual travels, which are those of the intellectual detective: he finds clues, makes lists, and suddenly synthesizes this information. Thus, *Call for the Dead* turns on the following passage:

> As he stood gazing at the little shepherdess, poised eternally between her two admirers, he realized dispassionately that there was another quite different solution, ... a solution which matched every detail of circumstance, reconciled the nagging inconsistencies ... the realization began as an academic exercise without reference to personalities; Smiley maneuvered the characters like pieces in a puzzle, twisting them this way and that to fit the complex framework of established facts—and then, in a moment, the pattern had suddenly re-formed with such assurance that it was a game no more.

The detective element remains with Smiley through all of his adventures. He must detect the mole at the Circus in *Tinker, Tailor,* he must discover why Moscow pays Drake Ko such large sums of money in *The Honourable Schoolboy,* and in *Smiley's People* he must unravel the reason that Soviet hoods have been bothering Maria Ostrakova. He does solve all of the problems, but like most fictional British detectives since the late 1920s (Sayers's Peter Wimsey, for example), Smiley always finds, to his grief, that the hunt must end in the kill and that the kill can be bloody, senseless, and obscene. But this gets too far ahead of the argument.

The introduction of the term academic, as in the passage above, holds much for le Carré, and in his novels he uses it not only as a general description of people and behavior, but he also explores its real application to the intelligence community. George Smiley belongs to the older generation of intelligence workers from a time when the spy establishment was founded and run by true academics. Le Carré frequently goes through the litany of the founders' names. There was Jebedee, Smiley's tutor at Oxford.

There was Fielding, the French medievalist from Cambridge, Sparke from the school of Oriental languages, and Steed-Asprey who had been dining at High Table the night Smiley had been Jebedee's guest.

During the war, le Carré tells us, spying grew out of the academy, it was an amateur enterprise, it has traditional associations, it was upper class and unorthodox, and it died when the war ended:

> Gone for ever were the days of Steed-Asprey, when like as not you took your orders over a glass of port in his rooms at Magdalen; the inspired amateurism of a handful of highly qualified, under-paid men had given way to the efficiency, bureaucracy and intrigue of a large government department.

This passage gets us to the institutional theme which I will take up later, but it also cements Smiley in with the older generation of academic humanists who temporarily became spies to serve their country and their ideals. From the start le Carré feels that the academic side of Smiley, not just the quality of his mind, needs to be emphasized. In introducing us to his hero, the narrator of *Call for the Dead* says that he

> dreamed of fellowships and a life devoted to the literary obscurities of seventeenth-century Germany. But his own tutor, who knew Smiley better, guided him wisely away from the honours that would undoubtedly have been his.

The word "wisely" here suggests that Smiley will be able to achieve selfhood in the conflict and spiritual tensions of espionage, whereas the purely academic life will give him only static nonentity. Smiley, however, never goes far from the academe in his new profession as a spy. In the history which le Carré builds for him we learn that, after Oxford, Smiley taught in Germany and that directly after the war he, like the other dons turned spy, left the Circus and returned to Oxford to teach and do research. Throughout the novels Smiley continues his involvement with German baroque literature, and characters frequently mistake him for a schoolmaster. The school, as we will see later, assumes a vital metaphoric role in these novels. On the character level, though, it affects Smiley because an essential part of him is a teacher. Particularly in *Call for the Dead* and *The Honourable Schoolboy,* le Carré includes Smiley's students, Frey and Westerby, in the plots in order to bring out the intellectual and emotional complexities and paradoxes implicit in the teacher-student relationship.

Smiley also lives with the complexities and paradoxes of his marriage to Lady Ann Sercomb. This is a match of Beauty and the Beast, the Princess and the Toad. Smiley's Ann, aristocratic and painfully beautiful, takes up a life of philandering from the second sentence of *Call for the Dead*. She runs off with a Cuban race car driver, and, as the books proceed, fills her dance card with myriad names—including that of Bill Haydon, Moscow's spy at the Circus. Yet, from the end of the first novel to the scene in the middle of *Smiley's People* (the only place in the canon where she actually appears), she always returns to Smiley seeking reconciliation. From an objective viewpoint, Ann is a tart and Smiley is a besotted cuckold for indulging her in her infidelities. Yet in the novels she represents more than this. She stands for Smiley's unwilling and masochistic relationship with conventional, upper-class life. The question "How's Ann?" reminds readers of Smiley's separation from people like Saul Enderby or Roddy Martindale. Ann, moreover, stands for a variety of human contacts which Smiley wants and needs but cannot achieve. This stands out when le Carré describes Smiley's relationship with Mendel in *Call for the Dead*:

> It was four o'clock. They sat for a while talking in a rather desultory way about bees and housekeeping, Mendel quite at ease and Smiley still bothered and awkward, trying to find a way of talking, trying not to be clever. He could guess what Ann would have said about Mendel. She would have loved him, made a person of him, had a special voice and face for imitating him, would have made a story of him until he fitted into their lives and wasn't a mystery any more. . . . "Toad, do ask him to dinner. You must. Not to giggle at but to *like*."

This part of Ann, Smiley realizes, is half artificial—he realizes that she would soon dismiss Mendel from her consciousness—but he craves her easy sociability. He also needs Ann's perceptive and definite analyses of his own personal dilemmas—

> Only Ann, though she could not read his workings, refused to accept his findings. She was quite passionate, in fact, as only women can be on matters of business, really driving him to go back, take up where he had left off, never to veer aside in favour of the easy arguments.

Finally, Ann's continued presence represents for Smiley the goal of love. Le Carré never makes this point mawkishly; indeed, in *Call for the Dead*, he belittles it at the end of the novel, referring to Smiley's return to Ann as "the pathetic quest for love." Yet this Sisyphean quest, which lasts through the middle of *Smiley's People,* is superior to the quest for the "black grail," one's enemies, Karla.

That Smiley possesses the sensitivity to realize his equivocal positions is another main point in his character. Coming, as I have said, from the Golden Age detective hero, Smiley combines acumen with human sympathy. In *A Murder of Quality,* the narrator tells us that "once in the war he had been described by his superiors as possessing the cunning of Satan and the conscience of a virgin." Just as Karla provides a contrast to evoke Smiley's humanity in the later novels, Mendel provides one in *Call for the Dead.* As a policeman, Mendel accepts that his job requires him to deal with "the squalor" of criminals and the criminal mind, and he ignores the causes of deviant behavior because his role requires him to expunge the effects of human wickedness. Smiley, on the other hand, also deals with the effects of wickedness, but he always acknowledges and grieves for the causes. He steps out of the role of George Smiley and tries to see what others see and feel what others feel. Interviewing a woman who later turns out to be a communist agent, Smiley goes beyond the hunt and analyzes himself as the hunter: "Smiley felt suddenly sick and cheap. Loyalty to whom, to what? She didn't sound resentful. He was the oppressor." Very clearly le Carré attaches the term "toad" to Smiley. This works as an antiheroic physical description, but it has a mental referent too. Smiley is Mr. Toad from *Wind in the Willows,* constantly becoming other people, and refusing the domestic comforts of Toad Hall for the arduous life of the road. He has the unique capacity for being not only himself but also being everybody. Le Carré makes this fact clear with the self-consciously over-blown rhetoric in *Smiley's People,* when the Superintendent reflects upon his encounter with Smiley:

> Not one face at all actually, the Superintendent reflected. . . . More your whole range of faces. More your patchwork of different ages, people, and endeavours. Even—thought the Superintendent—of different faiths. . . .
>
> An Abbey, the Superintendent decided. That's what he was, an abbey. . . . An abbey, made up of all sorts of conflicting ages and styles and convictions.

Smiley can be everybody and be himself—indeed he needs to be everyone to be himself, just as Fitzgerald needs to be himself and Gatsby. If Smiley is not quite Shakespeare's "heavenly mingle" of Rome and Alexandria, or Arnold's wished-for synthesis of old and new, he is the only character in le

Carré who can stand between two worlds and, if not reconcile them, live with the opposites thrust upon him by life.

In the last two novels, however, le Carré shows the dissolution of Smiley's abbey. Unlike the eternally youthful adventure hero of the conventional spy book, Smiley, never young, grows older in the novels. With age he loses his ability to respond to life in a private and flexible manner. At the end of *The Honourable Schoolboy* he admits as much in a letter to Ann:

> Today, all I know is that I have learned to interpret the whole of life in terms of conspiracy. That is the sword I have lived by, and as I look round me now I see it is the sword I shall die by as well. These people terrify me, but I am one of them.

In *Smiley's People*, George moves from the multifaceted human being to the single-minded one. Whereas in his first encounter with Karla, the Russian spy-master (described in *Tinker, Tailor*), Smiley projected himself onto Karla, in the last novel quite the opposite happens and Smiley, as a logical but depressing consequence of their competition, becomes the remorseless gamester just when Karla proves that he *is* like Smiley. In doing this Smiley cuts himself off from Ann, refusing the invitation she offers in the middle of the novel. He wins Karla's defection, but loses himself; he, like Antony, goes over to Rome and betrays his heart. Smiley, in *Smiley's People*, moves from between two worlds, but in so doing he loses the humanity which he possessed. All he has left is his painful consciousness—as in the Hardy poem "I Look into My Glass":

> I look into my glass
> And view my wasting skin,
> And say, "Would God it came to pass
> My heart had shrunk as thin."
>
> (ll. 1–4)

But Smiley is just one man. As old Craw says in *The Honourable Schoolboy*:

> "The old order changes not, let it run on. You won't stop the wheel—not together, not divided—you snivelling, arse-licking novices! You're a bunch of suicidal tits to try."

The wheel represents the fundamental change of human existence, but it also stands for the force of humans acting in concert through the institution. The people in le Carré live and work in institutions which give them roles and often subsume their uniqueness. Drawing the institution, therefore, becomes of utmost importance to le Carré and his fictions, not only in order to present his spies' worlds fully and realistically, but also to delineate problems of human behavior. In a 1977 interview le Carré described the world of the Circus as "a microcosm of all institutional behavior, and the ever-repeated dilemma which overcomes individuals when they submit their talent for institutional exploitation." To a far greater extent than Cheyney or Fleming or Deighton or Hall or Haggard, le Carré brings the institution of the Circus across to his readers. First, he gives it local habitation and a name. His spy organization is not a series of initials (M.I.6; WOOCP; etc.) but a nickname, bringing it more intimately to our attention. It resides in an Edwardian building on Cambridge Circus in London. Especially in *The Honourable Schoolboy* le Carré renders a sense of place, describing the torn-up walls, the piles of plaster, and the litter of papers. Although he does not describe them in detail, le Carré gives readers the impression that the Circus is, really, the headquarters of an extensive institution. Once again he does this by giving name, or nickname, and location—

> the Sarratt Nursery . . . the experimental audio laboratories in
> Harlow; the stinks-and-bangs school in Argyll; the water school
> in the Helford Estuary . . . the long-arm radio-transmission base
> at Canterbury . . . [and] the wranglers' headquarters in Bath,
> where the code-breaking went on.

Once le Carré hooks readers by the places, he dips them into a world of professional jargon. We find le Carré speaking of lamplighters, babysitters, scalp-hunters, yellow-perils, sound-thieves, ferrets, honey traps, bugger-all, cousins, etc. These draw us further into the secret world and through them le Carré also shows how people within institutions invent their own jargon, not to communicate more effectively but to cut themselves off from the outside world (in *Smiley's People*, George, retired for some months, has to ask the meaning of "bugger-all"), and also to humanize their own inhuman realm through inventing nicknames. Le Carré knew his Orwell. For the same purposes he shows the jargon extended to a special, insiders' language when Jerry speaks Red Indian to Smiley in *Tinker, Tailor*, and with Craw's Vaticanese in *The Honourable Schoolboy*.

Unlike other spy writers, who concern themselves only with the present moment of their secret bureaus, le Carré weaves the history of the Circus through his novels. He, of course, ties this history to changing internal and international climates in Britain, but most of his attention goes to the personalities of the administrators who reflect the changes on a personal level. During the war, the Circus was run by academics, Fielding, Jebedee, Sparke,

Steed-Asprey, and Landsburg (added in *A Murder of Quality*). During this era, le Carré suggests, the Circus thrived because of the heroic state of the nation and the genuine class, brains, wit, and amateur status of its leaders. In *Call for the Dead* we meet the first postwar chief of the Circus, one Maston. Maston dithers over issues, fawns on Ministers and M.P.'s, and lets his own people down:

> It comforted the Great to deal with a man they knew, a man who could reduce any colour to grey, who knew his masters and could walk among them. And he did it so well. They liked his diffidence when he apologized for the company he kept, his insincerity when he defended the vagaries of his subordinates, his flexibilities when formulating new commitments. Nor did he let go the advantages of a cloak and dagger man *malgré lui,* wearing the cloak for his masters and preserving the dagger for his servants.

Not only is Maston the complete bureaucrat, he lacks class: Smiley brands him as "a barmaid's dream of a real gentleman." With *The Spy Who Came In from the Cold* le Carré cans Maston and brings in Control as the head of the Circus. Control has a bit of the old school about him: he is upper-class, dreadfully efficient, and a former don. Unlike the old academics who were brilliant, jovial, and open, Control is the irascible scholar who works in secret and bitterly attacks what he perceives to be folly. Control is the spy's spy, the fictional cliché, holding all of the threads, coolly analyzing human motives, playing the Great Game successfully with his nation's enemies. He may get things done, but he is at first a sinister figure (in *The Spy Who Came In from the Cold*) and then, in *Tinker, Tailor,* he becomes a pathetic individual, cut off from his fellows, alone in a world of paranoia. After Control's death in *Tinker, Tailor,* the mantle passes to shallow, middle-class Percy Alleline. According to the Circus rumor mill, Alleline had been Control's student at Cambridge, "and a bad one." Maston recruited him to the Circus—thereby linking him to the bureaucratic type—where he achieved some success through his "faculty of bullish persuasion." Alleline possessed a "fatal reverence for the Americans" which caused him to flub a job in Egypt and landed him in a desk job. From there he used his political influence to promote himself to a more influential job, and from this job, Moscow Center gave him the material to oust Control and take his job—because he was a nincompoop. After the fall of Alleline and his Svengali, Bill Haydon, Smiley becomes the head of the Circus in *The Honourable Schoolboy,* and he proves to be a master of intelligence technique. In the same novel, however, Smiley as a leader and administrator loses to Saul Enderby and Sam Collins.

These two, who take over the Circus in *Smiley's People,* are politicians in latter-day Britain who believe that the path to strength lies in falling in with the Americans, as opposed to Control who "despised them and all their works." This is also the sword by which they perish, for in *Smiley's People* Parliament has caught the fever for open government from the United States, has axed many of the Circus's functions, and is considering alteration of the Official Secrets Act on the pattern of the Freedom of Information Act in the U.S. Although he is not part of the Circus, Oliver Lacon shows the contemporary decline of the service. Acting as liaison with the Cabinet, Lacon helps, albeit fussily, to unmask the mole in *Tinker, Tailor.* In *The Honourable Schoolboy* he sits on the fence, neutrally observing events, unsure of which way power will move. By *Smiley's People,* though, he has become a eunuch.

Although there are variations within them, from this organizational history emerge two types. The first type, which encompasses Lacon, Maston, Alleline, Enderby, and Control, plays the game and will do anything to win. Granted, for Control, winning may have some international or doctrinal significance, but winning counts more than anything. For the others, and especially for Leclerc in *The Looking Glass War,* winning means perpetuating one's place and one's institution, and staying in power regardless of the cost in life or the damage done to one's personality by pandering. The second type is different; Smiley is different. Power means little to Smiley, enacted in his repeated retirements and resignations. When Michael Maccoby describes "the craftsman" in his book, *The Gamesman: The New Corporate Leaders,* he also gives a fairly accurate picture of Smiley's executive character:

> The craftsman holds the traditional values of the productive-hoarding character—the work ethic, respect for people, concern for quality and thrift. When he talks about his work his interest is in the *process* of making something; he enjoys building. He sees others, co-workers as well as superiors, in terms of whether they help or hinder him in doing a craftsmanlike job. Most of the craftsmen whom we interviewed are quiet, sincere, modest, and practical. . . . Although his virtues are admired by everyone, his self-containment and perfectionism do not allow him to lead a complex and changing organization. Rather than engaging and trying to master the system with the cooperation of others who share his values, he tends to do his own thing and go along, sometimes reluctantly, toward goals he does not share, enjoying whatever opportunities he finds for interesting work.

All of this describes Smiley with fair accuracy, except, perhaps, the last sentence. George does try to convince others of his values—especially Jerry in *The Honourable Schoolboy*—and he only goes along so far with those who do not share his values. Thus he quits the Circus after the war, after the action of *Call for the Dead* and after the action of *The Honourable Schoolboy*; in *Tinker, Tailor* and *Smiley's People,* in fact, Smiley is not a member of the Circus but an outsider. So far, however, the organization has always drawn Smiley back to it, because for Smiley it is more than a limited company peddling whalebone or jute. These products are as temporary as are presidents, controls, ministers, and agents. For Smiley the Circus is both a mundane organization and a transcendent one: it is a church and a school.

Whenever he introduces the subject of organizations in the novels, the metaphors of the church and the school abound. These are the transcendent institutions, in their ideal state, to which all other institutions aspire. In the novels the idea of the school plays a more important role, but le Carré does pointedly use the idea of the church to describe espionage institutions. From an organizational point of view, the church is a perfect corporate institution—not democratic sects but episcopal ones. It has a clear purpose, a desirable, even unique, product, a rigorous and clear organizational structure, and highly efficient means of motivating employee and consumer alike. Particularly in *The Looking Glass War,* le Carré uses the image of the church to enrich his portrayal of an organization. Here, the Department induces its members to view their employer in religious terms:

> For its servants, the Department had a religious quality. Like
> monks, they endowed it with a mystical identity far away from
> the hesitant, a sinful band which made up its ranks.

In this novel the members of a seedy espionage department boost their sense of purpose by consistently drawing parallels between their misdirected and fumbling business, and the church. The director becomes a primate elected by his fading connection with the glamor of World War II, and his priests lead Leiser through a purposely mysterious set of novitiate vows. To their confusion, the people in *The Looking Glass War* discover that their prelate is only a powerless cleric or even an unordained clerk (Leclerc) and that their faith rests on a past which is absolutely dead and the illusion of the non-existent Soviet missiles. This novel dwells upon the irony of forcing the mundane and temporal into the exalted and spiritual realm of the church. But this does not mean that it cannot be done: *The Spy Who Came In from the Cold* shows this. Le Carré builds this novel on the contrast of Fiedler and Leamas: of British democracy and communist totalitarianism. Fiedler does his job for East German security because he believes in the reality of utopian Marxism. He is shocked by Leamas's lack of philosophy, and at the start of the novel Leamas has little knowledge of his own motives, beyond hatred. By the end of the book, though, he does, and we ought to see this in a religious framework. He realizes that London means something:

> They don't proselytize; they don't stand in pulpits or on party platforms and tell us to fight for Peace or for God or whatever it is. They're the poor sods who try to keep the preachers from blowing each other sky high.

This is pure le Carré: an antichurch devoted to keeping other faiths from destroying the world. This church takes "pansies, sadists and drunkards, people who play cowboys and Indians" and ennobles them by giving them a role in a transcendent institution. Many of its adherents leave it for other faiths, for it promises no victory, but unremitting toil. Only George Smiley tries to live up to the destructive discipline, and even he, as Jerry Westerby puts it, is a "failed cleric."

At one time in his life, the biographical notes tell us, John le Carré taught school at Eton College. Perhaps as a consequence of this (it *is*, after all, also a standard locale in the detective story), two of his books use public schools as locales: *A Murder of Quality* takes place at a major public school, and the Jim Prideaux sections of *Tinker, Tailor* occur at Thursgood's school. Both of these novels portray teachers and students and develop two of the countless variety of relationships which can develop between teacher and student. As we have seen, le Carré mirrors reality by making dons the founders of the Circus, and he makes his major character, George Smiley, an academic and former teacher. Further, just as the church as a metaphor illuminates the world of espionage organizations, the school as an idea has a great deal to do with the secret world in le Carré.

Behind the use of the school metaphor lies the assumption that the Circus as an institution performs the same function that the school does. Behind Smiley's predicaments in all of the novels rests the fact that the Circus and the school serve two sets of goals which can become contradictory and mutually destructive, given sets of perverse circumstances and the errant nature of human beings. As institutions, cultures create schools for a number of practical reasons. Schools train people for jobs, they insure cultural continuity and a smoothly running society, and they produce theoretical knowledge needed for practical things—from divorce counselling sessions to lasers. But they play another role as well. Schools aim at preparing people for life, at passing on the accumulated wisdom of mankind, and at seeking out knowledge regardless of its impact on society. Schools try to awaken individuals to their own and others' humanity, they try to harbor and protect the true and beautiful, and they strive to teach people how to become their own teachers.

As le Carré depicts the Circus in his novels, it fulfills some of the same functions as the school. First, it serves the specific culture that created it, servile to the culture's wishes and objectives. It also, like any other intelligence agency, collates, interprets, and publishes information. Leclerc in *The Looking Glass War*, Connie and Di Salis in *The Honourable Schoolboy,* and Smiley in all of his novels, engage in pursuits identical to one kind of scholarship which collects and analyzes information. If Leclerc is deluded as an individual it is, in large measure, because he is a bad scholar and handles information dishonestly. If the academic historian needs to be careful in his interpretation of facts, so does the intelligence officer: le Carré insists on the spy-historian analogy through the point of view which he adopts in the novels. Not only do schools and spies gather information, they both train individuals in useful skills. In *The Looking Glass War* we see an ironic contrast between the real academe and the spy school when Haldane and Avery set up their one-horse training school in a house near Oxford. The Circus's training school for agents comes into most of the novels, but it plays a vital role in *The Honourable Schoolboy* where Jerry, cut loose in Hong Kong, thinks again and again of the material at Sarratt. There agents learn how to shadow, how to rendezvous, how to kill. Following through on the education analogy, the Circus's function is to serve its society. It may proselytize for budget but it does not develop policy: it has no ideas. Obviously, what le Carré presents us with here is a sterile machine dealing in dead or deadly information and devoted to death and not life. Countless schools do this, too: they enslave and neuter the human spirit rather than liberating it.

Schools, though, can develop in another direction. In *The Honourable Schoolboy,* le Carré exploits the ideals of the school to a greater degree than in any of the other novels: part of its structure and much of its characterization depends upon the academic comparison. What le Carré suggested all along about Smiley becomes apparent here—he was and will always be a schoolmaster. The other characters in *The Honourable Schoolboy* grow from their relationship with Smiley as the schoolmaster. Connie and Di Salis are his staff and the other men are his students. Smiley administers, educates, plans courses of study, and attempts discipline. Le Carré includes in the novel two interview scenes with Westerby and Collins which feel very much like the boy's interview with the headmaster in the schoolboy novel. He also portrays his major characters as clearly defined schoolboy types. Guillam is the upperclassman who dependably does routine chores for the headmaster.

Fawn is the fawning brown-noser whose viciousness is subdued only by the sense of authority which he gains from dogging the master's steps. Sam Collins is the dishonorable schoolboy who, rumor has it, cheated rather than worked his way through Oxford. During the course of *The Honourable Schoolboy,* Collins prefers maneuvering and scheming to forthrightness and hard work, adopting the manners and the ethics of the casino which he runs during his rustication. Jerry Westerby is, on the other hand, the honorable schoolboy. No genius, Jerry seems to be loud-mouthed athlete turned mediocre reporter in *Tinker, Tailor.* In the next novel, however, le Carré shows that Westerby learned something from Smiley beyond tradecraft. He puts into action the ideals which George only teaches. Le Carré, in *The Honourable Schoolboy,* brings Smiley and Westerby close together. He does this particularly through the descriptions of Ann Smiley and Lizzie Worth. Both Smiley and Jerry have failed marriages and they love the same sort of women. Both Ann and Lizzie are irresponsible, and both have affairs with brainless Latin he-men (Ann's first infidelity is with a Cuban race car driver and Lizzie's is with the Mexican, Tiny Ricardo, ace aviator). However worthless these women seem, the pursuit of them represents the heroes' striving for the spontaneous, human side of life. This is the parallel between Smiley and Jerry and it operates through the metaphor of the school. Education, when it works, should liberate people and make them their own teachers: thinkers as diverse as Nietzsche and Leonardo have insisted that the student who cannot surpass his master has failed him. In *Call for the Dead* Smiley comes close to despair because one of his former students, Dieter Frey, has betrayed his education:

> Everything he [Smiley] admired or loved had been the product of
> intense individualism. That was why he hated Dieter now, hated
> what he stood for more strongly than before: it was the fabulous
> impertinence of renouncing the individual in favour of the mass.
> When had mass philosophies ever brought benefit or wisdom?
> Dieter cared nothing for human life: dreamed only of armies of
> faceless men bound by their lowest common denominator.

With Jerry Westerby, though, Smiley wins. Jerry's quixotic love for Lizzie and his attempts to protect the Ko brothers define him. He weighs the opposites (Lizzie is a whore and Drake Ko is a thug; he loves Lizzie and the Kos' love is admirable) and acts to protect the ideal. This enables Smiley and the reader to honor him. George cannot give himself to Ann, and, as *Smiley's People* shows, he cannot protect the human side of a wicked person even if he values this humanness. He may not be able to make the leap of faith, but he can and does prepare Jerry for it, and Smiley succeeds because Jerry surpasses him.

In terms of plot, le Carré began and, in a sense, remains a detective story writer instead of an adventure writer. His *A Murder of Quality* reminds us that le Carré was interested in the detective story form, and this is evident when we examine his spy plots—particularly the early ones. *Call for the Dead* may deal with international intrigue but it is a detective novel. In it le Carré introduces clues, shows the detective compiling lists, and shows the detective's moment of insight but withholds the name of the guilty party until the action climaxes. Here, too, he uses a detective writer's device as old as Christie's first novel, *The Mysterious Affair at Styles* (1920), the device of raising suspicion, then dismissing it, and then demonstrating guilt. *The Spy Who Came In from the Cold,* likewise, grows out of detective plotting. Here, in the flip-flops on Mundt's allegiance, le Carré only modifies the guilty-innocent-guilty technique of the first novel. In this novel le Carré also provides clues to the readers for the solution of the plot: Smiley's brief but ominous appearance in the early part of the narrative. Le Carré, in *The Spy Who Came In from the Cold,* does more than write a detective plot with espionage trappings. Through his creation of atmosphere, character, and dialogue le Carré takes us out of the make-believe world of detective fiction and thrusts us into the grubby world of the cellars of international politics. We can more easily believe in the double cross—the accusation of Mundt in order to clear him—when it occurs in the grimy realm of political jockeying than we can believe in the double cross in the pastoral setting of the traditional detective novel. Further, le Carré in this novel ties the plot not to the intellectual game, but to the inversion of values which we find in all of his novels: if Mundt is evil to the East Germans he is good to the West regardless of his moral worth.

After *The Spy Who Came In from the Cold,* le Carré stopped trying to plot his novels as writer-reader detective stories with clues planted for us to see and a trick at the end. In *A Small Town in Germany* he switched types of hero, and made Alan Turner the hard-boiled detective who uncovers facts because he crashes into events and people. He does, granted, give us a prologue showing Leo tracking Karfeld, but *A Small Town in Germany* does not have the clue orientation or the trick ending of the previous novels: le Carré does not invite us to guess about guilt or the solution. After *A Small Town in Germany* the only remnant of detective technique in the plotting of his novels lies in the fact that le Carré constructs his books by hoarding information and dribbling it out to the readers. He knows all of the facts which create the ending and could give them to the readers early on, but instead he doles the facts out one at a time in order to unfold the plot through gained knowledge rather than, say, adventure. In the early novels, when tied to other plot devices, this creates detective stories, while in the later books, when coupled with the narrator's voice, it contributes to the aura of history which le Carré intentionally weaves into his books.

From the very first chapter that he wrote, le Carré slanted his espionage novels toward history: the opening chapter of *Call for the Dead* is "A Brief History of Mr. George Smiley." As we have seen, as one of his main objects le Carré writes the history of his imaginary spy organization from World War II to the present. More than anything else, the point of view in the novels pushes us toward a historical perspective. The narrator in le Carré is a detached observer who tries to piece together reality out of certain, known fragments. He follows leads into the distant past, into disparate locales, and into known fragments of people's lives. He deals with rumors and gossip— especially when concerned with Smiley's marriage. At the start of *The Honourable Schoolboy,* the narrator runs through a number of theories about the historical origins of the Dolphin case, and then proceeds to report a truer history. Like a responsible historian the narrator refuses to draw conclusions where there are no facts. Thus at the end of *The Honourable Schoolboy* he gives us the following statement:

> Was there really a conspiracy against Smiley of the scale that Guillam supposed? If so, how was it affected by Westerby's own maverick intervention? No information is available and even those who trust each other well are not disposed to discuss the question.

This ties in with the root assumption in le Carré: we cannot really know other people who are forever locked in themselves. All we can know is the external history, but we, as individuals, ought to have the insight not to ask about December 25, but to ask the essential but factually unanswerable question about whether Christ, or love, or truth existed at all. In asking that question we move toward making them exist.

Like Conrad or like Greene, le Carré uses the espionage form for wider human purposes than those present in the adventure story. The world of espionage, for him, intensifies the human condition and highlights questions of identity and existence. In the novels about the Circus we glimpse a perplexing and frightening world, but still a world in which choice operates and in which individuals can find themselves and touch other people. Le Carré possesses considerable narrative talents which we can see when comparing his Cambodia in *The Honourable Schoolboy* to Adam Hall's Cambodia in *The Kobra Manifesto* (1976). With him we can observe a trivial genre like the spy novel used to enrich mainstream literature.

ABRAHAM ROTHBERG

The Decline and Fall of George Smiley:
John le Carré and English Decency

Beginning with Rudyard Kipling's *Kim,* published virtually at the outset of this century, whose hero loved to play "The Great Game [of espionage] which never stops night or day," the twentieth century spawned in the spy perhaps the most popular of its fictional heroes. Of present-day writers of spy novels, none has achieved wider readership, or more serious attention, than has John le Carré. An Englishman whose real name is David Cornwell, le Carré was born during the Depression, was a schoolboy during World War II, and came of age during the 1950s, when public recognition of Britain's loss of power and prestige was made manifest in its defeat at Suez by new postwar superpowers, the United States and the Soviet Union. Only a little more than half a century after a time when the sun never set on the British Empire, le Carré's hero, George Smiley, represents a quite different view of British power and prospects from Kipling's Kim.

It is a tribute to le Carré's imagination, as well as one of his greatest limitations, that his hero's character can only be apprehended—if it can be apprehended at all—over the space of seven novels. Unless one has read all of them, it is difficult to glean any but the most rudimentary idea of the sort of man George Smiley is supposed to be; and even after one has read all the novels, not only his temperament and motivation, but the very facts of his life remain ill defined. This is a doubly damning failure in grasp and technique because obviously le Carré wishes us to consider George Smiley the

From *Southwest Review* 66, no. 4 (Autumn 1981). © 1981 by Southern Methodist University Press.

epitome of the best England has to offer; Smiley's decline and fall over those seven volumes is depicted not only as the defeat of an individual, but as the downfall of those virtues in British life for which he stands, and by implication demonstrates the causes of the decline and fall of British power and prestige. As le Carré's paragon of English decency, Smiley lives amidst the corruptions of Whitehall's politics and the machinations of British intelligence, and it is essential to recognize that le Carré's purpose is not merely to contrast Smiley's decency and probity with the want of principle and abuse of public trust by both politicians and spies, but also to compare Smiley's sagacity, sensitivity, and effectiveness with their stupidity, callousness, and ineptitude. Le Carré treats "the British secret services for what they surely are: microcosms of the British condition, of . . . [British] social attitudes and vanities." The picture he draws of intelligence organizations in his revealing introduction to *Philby: The Spy Who Betrayed a Generation* is even more explicit than that in his novels, but no more devastating. He sees the secret services as themselves without politics or ideology and incapable of understanding them in others. He believes the intelligence agencies to be filled only with "posturing chauvinism" and "The Establishment's easy trick of rationalising selfish decisions and dressing them in the clothes of a higher cause." Members of the intelligence services are recruited from the establishment by those who put "loyalty above intelligence; and pedigree above originality." Not only do such people identify class with loyalty, but they identify the good of the country with their own interests and the bureaucratic interests of the secret services. Flawed in such serious ways and improperly supervised, intelligence "sinks swiftly into intrigue, slovenly security and interdepartmental rivalry." Le Carré indicts the intelligence agencies, but he holds the society at large responsible as well:

> If the secret services were negligent in controlling Philby, so Parliament and we ourselves, society at large, were equally negligent in controlling the secret services. It was *our* politicians who fronted for them, *our* editors who suppressed for them, *our* dons who informed for them, recruited for them; *our* Prime Ministers who protected them.

I am, therefore, going to attempt to create a composite portrait of George Smiley not only by what le Carré says of him in the various novels, but specifically what le Carré has Smiley do in three of them: his first novel, *Call for the Dead*; the "middle" novel, *Tinker, Tailor, Soldier, Spy*; and the final book, *Smiley's People*. As le Carré develops Smiley's character from the early novels to the later, Smiley shifts from approval or at least forgiveness of personal and political betrayal to an inability and refusal to forgive and forget such treachery; he moves from his contingent and ambiguous loyalties to institutions to a loyalty only to his own standards and ideals.

If he finds something compulsive and anarchic in political and sexual betrayal, an undermining of the very foundations of society, le Carré also shows us almost every kind of personal loyalty as well: of parent for child, of husband for wife, of lover for lover, brother for brother, friend for friend. In this notion of the serving and redeeming power of love, there is a romanticism that runs through all le Carré's novels, an echo of Evelyn Waugh's Tony Last and Ford Madox Ford's Tietjens. If le Carré had chosen and been able to focus on Smiley's character in the kind of saga so brilliantly exemplified in Ford's *Parade's End,* he might have written a major novel of his own time.

In le Carré's first novel, *Call for the Dead,* the very first chapter is appropriately entitled "A Brief History of George Smiley," and its first line tells us:

> When Lady Ann Sercomb married George Smiley towards the end of the war [World War II], she described him to her astonished Mayfair friends as breathtakingly ordinary. When she left him two years later in favor of a Cuban motor racing driver, she announced enigmatically that if she hadn't left him then, she could never have done [so].

If Lady Ann is enigmatic here, so too is le Carré, for we never learn just why she did leave him, or why, if she hadn't just then, she never could have. Moreover, we never are shown what the roots of Ann's apparently obsessive promiscuity were, or what kept Smiley's love and fidelity constant, or, for that matter, why two such disparate people married in the first place; but the breakup of Smiley's marriage and the recurrent infidelities involved are a reiterated theme. With it, le Carré announces one of his most powerful and persistent concerns, the conflicts between loyalty and betrayal, setting it first in the context of a marriage before broadening it to the loyalties and treasons to the group, the class, the nation.

Short, fat, quiet, George Smiley looks like a "shrunken toad"—later we learn that "Toad" is one of Lady Ann's pet names for him—and is also "without school, parents, regiment or trade, without wealth or poverty." Smiley is an intelligence officer, a profession, we are told, which "provided him with what he had once loved best in life: academic excursions into the mystery of human behaviour, disciplined by the practical application of his own deductions." We first meet Smiley in the year 1943. He has already been an intelligence officer for sixteen years or more since a "sweet July morning in 1928," when just out of the "murky cloisters of his unimpressive Oxford College," he found his plans to devote himself to studying obscure seventeenth-century German writers diverted by a number of his most eminent teachers, who recruited him into the British Secret Service. Just why Smiley is impelled to go into intelligence work is unclear, but in performing that work, his feelings "were mixed and irreconcilable."

Smiley taught and studied in Germany and then, with his knowledge of German and Germans, was for four years a spy in Nazi Germany during World War II before being recalled to England in 1943. By that time, his superiors thought him worn out and dismissed him from the service. Smiley married the Lady Ann and took her back to Oxford, once more to devote himself to seventeenth-century German literature; but two years later, in 1945, after Ann had run off with her Cuban driver and after "the revelations of a young Russian cypher clerk in Ottawa," Smiley was recalled to British Intelligence. But the organization had changed. The men who had recruited Smiley were either dead or retired, and the one who remained was Maston, "the professional civil servant from an orthodox department, a man to handle paper and integrate the brilliance of his staff with the cumbersome machinery of bureaucracy." The "inspired amateurism" was over, the "glory" gone; what was left was Maston, "the NATO alliance, and the desperate measures contemplated by the Americans [which] altered the whole nature of Smiley's Service." Too old to go out into the field again, Smiley considered himself passed by, felt that "he had entered middle age without ever being young"; by then, Smiley was probably thirty-nine years old.

The action of *Call for the Dead* begins about a decade later, some time after 1956, though le Carré gives no specific date. Smiley is sent to interrogate a Foreign Office employee named Samuel Arthur Fennan because an anonymous letter has denounced Fennan as having been a Communist when he was an undergraduate at Oxford in the 1930s. Smiley interviews Fennan and clears him; when Fennan is shortly thereafter found dead, presumably a suicide, Maston asks Smiley to look into it. From the very first, Smiley is uneasy with the assignment, feels "sick and cheap" about investigating Fennan's loyalty. "Loyalty to whom, to what?" he asks himself, questions that will echo through the ensuing novels, though he knows that Fennan's job at the Foreign Office gave him access to important government documents. When Fennan's wife accuses Smiley of having caused her husband's death, le Carré introduces one of his major themes, the conflict between personal and larger loyalties, especially between those to the individual and to the state.

Maston wants the suicide verdict accepted, the file closed, so that no hint of scandal will attach to the Foreign Office or security services. He insists on quashing the investigation, but since Smiley cannot convince himself that Fennan committed suicide, he writes Maston a note of resignation. So begins Smiley's role as the voice of reason, common sense, and decency in opposition to the coldheartedness, hypocrisy, and stupidity of the governmental bureaucracy. Smiley is also the defender of an independent and competent intelligence service which provides objective information whether it suits the domestic political conveniences of its "customers" or not. Le Carré has Smiley play both roles in every novel in which he appears.

Smiley is able "unofficially" to solve the crime, but in having him do so, le Carré employs the very long arm of not very likely coincidence.

Fennan, it seems, was murdered by a killer named Mundt. Attached to the East German Steel Commission in London, Mundt is part of a spy network run by Dieter Frey. Jewish, crippled, but "beautiful" despite his deformity, Frey, it turns out, was Smiley's student in prewar Germany. During the war, Smiley recruited Frey into his espionage network and Frey became his best agent, daring, resourceful, dedicated. After the war, Frey, who "hated the Americans," became an East German agent and later recruited Mrs. Fennan. When Smiley and Inspector Mendel track Frey down, Frey attempts to kill Mendel; Smiley, blindly angry, half-accidentally knocks Dieter into the Thames, "offered like a human sacrifice to the London fog and the foul black river lying beneath it." Filled with the "nausea of guilt," Smiley berates himself because Dieter "had let him do it, had not fired the gun, had remembered their friendship when Smiley had not."

Le Carré's (and Smiley's) consistent fascination with and admiration for the absolutists of the world is here manifest for the first but by no means the last time. "Dieter," Smiley avers, "mercurial, absolute, had fought to build a civilization. Smiley, rationalistic, protective, had fought to prevent him. 'Oh God,' said Smiley aloud, 'who was then the gentleman . . . ?'"

The conclusion le Carré wishes us to draw is that Smiley committed a crime, but the actions of the novel contradict that or at least call it into serious question. It was, after all, Dieter Frey who ran an intelligence operation against Smiley's country in the course of which he was responsible for having Mundt attack Smiley and murder a car-rental agent; also, Dieter himself attempted to murder Inspector Mendel and actually did murder Mrs. Fennan with his own hands. What le Carré is doing here, I believe, is proposing the same answer to the conflict between personal and communal loyalties that E. M. Forster had done in his famous (and infamous) declaration: "I hate the idea of causes, and if I had to choose between betraying my country and betraying my friend, I hope I should have the guts to betray my country." (Forster wrote that in 1939, when such treachery would have meant betraying England to the Nazis.)

Just as Forster had evidently not considered whether betraying one's country also included betraying more than one individual friend, betraying an entire community of one's friends and neighbors as well as the larger community that composes society, so, too, le Carré does not consider or resolve that dilemma, or even face it as squarely as, say, Sophocles had done more than two thousand years earlier in the *Antigone*. Moreover, he has not fictionally prepared us to accept Smiley's self-laceration as either appropriate or credible, for it is Dieter Frey who caused Samuel Fennan to denounce his wife as a spy, who caused Mrs. Fennan to betray not only the country which had offered her sanctuary after her persecutions at the hands of the Nazis, but also the husband she loves—ultimately to his death at the hands of the new East German authoritarians. Is such betrayal not personal enough? not political enough? And is it not far worse than the sexual betrayals of Smiley's Lady Ann?

Caught on the horns of this dilemma, Smiley's last words on Dieter Frey and Mrs. Fennan are, to say the least, misleading if not downright false. Mrs. Fennan "wanted to help build one society which could live without conflict. Peace is a dirty word now, isn't it?" Smiley says. "I think she wanted peace." And of Dieter he adds, "God knows what Dieter wanted. Honor, I think, and a socialist world. . . . They dreamed of peace and freedom. Now they're murderers and spies. . . . He was one of those world-builders who seem to do nothing but destroy." Aside from the illogicality of that last line, the words of the speech are almost communist slogans, and neither le Carré nor Smiley says anything to show the difference between dream and reality. Moreover, because the statements come at the very end of the novel, as a kind of eulogy, they seem to be an unbelievable and contradictory whitewash of the actions that have taken place earlier.

A note arrives from the Lady Ann in Zurich asking Smiley to take her back, "an offer no gentleman would accept," yet despite Smiley's recognition that the letter means only that Ann is saying, "I have wearied my lover, my lover has wearied me, let me shatter your world again: my own bores me," in the last paragraph of the novel he is flying to Switzerland for a reunion with her.

Surely, then, le Carré's finale is no victory of good over evil, of loyalty over treachery, of freedom over tyranny, or even of love over lust. In the world of the family, and the world at large, ambiguity and sheer confusion—not the least of which seems to be le Carré's—rule.

In *Tinker, Tailor, Soldier, Spy* (1974), le Carré is still concerned with the same matrix of problems he has explored before: the loss of British power and its effect on British life and the British establishment; the ambivalence and outright hatred involved in what used to be called the "special relationship" between the United Kingdom and the United States; the nature of loyalty; the reconciliation of ends and means. The action of the novel takes place some time in 1973, and is obviously based on the historic Kim Philby case, which gives le Carré the opportunity to develop further his criticisms of the British establishment and to explicate his reflections on the nature of fidelity and betrayal. With a confidence he seemed to lack in the earlier and more modest novels, le Carré now deals with the intelligence services as a microcosm of British society and as a metaphor for human life as a whole.

Le Carré's delineation of the establishment is scathing. Almost everyone in it is dedicated to self-aggrandizement and self-protection; almost everyone wants power, prestige, promotion, money; almost no one seems capable even of disinterestedness, much less of self-transcendence. A British ruling class is rigidly bound by class and ethnic biases, blinded by dreams of empire and grandeur, by fantasies about playing a larger role in international affairs than either the nation's health or its resources would warrant.

Yet a remnant is saved, or at least salvageable, led by that emblem of British decency, probity, and fairness, George Smiley. Once more out of the Secret Service, Smiley is recalled by Oliver Lacon, the parliamentary "watchdog of Intelligence affairs," to ferret out a long-term double agent—a so-called Soviet "mole"—who has penetrated the very highest echelons of British Intelligence. In the secret war, the focus has shifted from Germany to the Soviet Union; the Russian Intelligence Service headed by the pseudonymous Karla is now the enemy instead of the *Abteilung*, but in this novel the major conflict is not so much with the Soviets as with their British surrogate, their penetration agent, Bill Haydon, now the second in command in Smiley's service. Le Carré's depiction of the disarray in that service is relentless; naked ambition and petty rivalry rule and obscure, even deliberately ignore, the evidence and the threat to the security of the service and the nation. Only when a rogue agent forces the information that the Russians have a "mole" at the heart of British Intelligence on Oliver Lacon do he and his Minister bring Smiley in to track the "mole" down, but they do so reluctantly.

In ferreting out his "mole," Smiley explores the byways of various treasons and loyalties—to nation, to profession, to colleagues, to wives, lovers, and children. In Haydon, le Carré has an establishment figure who, like Philby, came from the right class, went to the right schools, had the right accent and manners, and could not therefore be presumed to have anything but the right allegiances. Because he is one of theirs, the establishment is prepared to make excuses for Bill Haydon, to look away from the incriminating facts—as in life it did for Philby—to say that he was, after all, an artist, or disappointed by the waning power of Britain. "Poor loves. Trained to Empire, trained to rule the waves. All gone. All taken away," Smiley's Soviet expert, Connie Sachs, remarks. Yet Haydon was recruited (as was Philby) long before Britain's weakness and hollowness were quite so evident or so acknowledged; and Haydon himself materially contributed to that weakness.

Behind Haydon, of course, is the Soviet absolutist Karla, whom Smiley had once long before tried to persuade to defect. Karla, detained in India and threatened with execution if he returned to the Soviet Union because several of his networks in the West were rolled up, does not yield to Smiley's attempts to win him over. Karla speaks not a word. Though a chain smoker of American cigarettes, he refuses all but one pack of Camels that Smiley offers him and keeps that pack unopened all during the night to demonstrate to himself and to Smiley his self-control, his will, his refusal to defect. Karla returns to the Soviet Union, is sent to Siberia, but is eventually what the Soviets call "rehabilitated" and rises to head the branch of military intelligence for which Haydon works.

In their Indian encounter, Karla takes a gold cigarette lighter Ann had given to Smiley engraved, "To George from Ann with all my love," and under the circumstances Smiley is unable to ask for it back. This symbolic act reverberates through *Tinker, Tailor* and *Smiley's People.* Smiley knows Karla to be a fanatic, even believes his "lack of moderation will be his downfall," but he admires Karla's refusal to defect—and le Carré wants us to admire it as well. Yet, when Smiley at last catches Haydon in the act, he makes all sorts of excuses for Haydon's defection—excuses which, evidently, le Carré expects us to find persuasive as well:

> Haydon had betrayed. As a lover, a colleague, a friend; as a patriot; as a member of that inestimable body that Ann loosely called the Set: in every capacity, Haydon had overtly pursued one aim and secretly achieved its opposite. . . . Yet there was a part of him [Smiley] that rose already in Haydon's defense. Was not Bill also betrayed? . . . He saw with painful clarity an ambitious man born to the big canvas, brought up to rule, divide and conquer, whose visions and vanities were fixed . . . upon the world's game; for whom the reality was a poor island with scarcely a voice that would carry across the water. Thus Smiley felt not only

disgust, but . . . a resentment against the institutions he was supposed to be protecting.

"The Minister's lolling mendacity, Lacon's tight-lipped moral complacency, the bludgeoning greed of Percy Alleline" invalidate the social contract for Smiley. "Why," he asks, "should anyone be loyal to them?"

Forgotten are two decades of treason, the deliberate destruction of the Secret Service, the death of at least three Russians and half a dozen Czechs. Though Smiley knows this and recognizes that Haydon is concealing valuable intelligence information, he cannot and does not press him. Moreover, Smiley listens without contradiction to Haydon's harangues against the United States, "no longer capable of undertaking its own revolution," and against Britain, whose political posture "is without relevance or moral viability in world affairs." Not until Haydon recounts his affair with the Lady Ann does Smiley react negatively, and in the circumstances relatively politely: "By then Smiley had had enough, so he slipped out, not bothering to say good-bye." Haydon had made it clear to Smiley that Ann was of no personal importance to him; going to bed with her was Karla's idea, because Karla had long since recognized Smiley as his chief antagonist in the Circus. "He said you were quite good," Haydon tells Smiley. "But you had this one price: Ann. The last illusion of the illusionless man. He reckoned that if I were known to be Ann's lover around the place, you wouldn't see me very straight when it came to other things." Ends and means in both senses, the warping of political and personal loyalties.

If, however, Haydon underestimates how straight Smiley will see him, le Carré overestimates how straight his reader can see George Smiley. The Smiley le Carré presents is vague, elusive, understated; all we see of him are gestures, tics, mannerisms, an occasional throwaway line: he wipes his glasses with the fat end of his tie; he is interested in German literature; he is always "a little embarrassed by protestations of anti-Communism" (why?); like one of his colleagues, he "had no real childhood" (why not?). Because le Carré is determined to create and sustain the narrative drive and tension of the thriller, he withholds essential information, important feelings, permits us only the most arbitrary and sometimes capricious access to his major character's mind and feeling. In so doing, le Carré imprisons himself in the form of the espionage novel, bars his own way to more serious fiction; if we knew how Smiley felt or thought, or how Ann or Haydon did, the action might be somewhat less suspenseful, but the characters would compel our belief.

Le Carré's characterization, therefore, attenuates the seriousness, scope, and impact of his novels. In delineating Smiley's love for his wife, le Carré rarely shows Smiley and Ann together, except in Smiley's recollection, through Smiley's eyes, and once removed in time and space. Nor does le Carré allow access to Ann's mind, so she remains as much a mystery as her marriage to Smiley and her penchant for bedding many men. Smiley, brilliant intelligence officer and interrogator, never seems quite able to solve that mystery, or talk to his wife freely and intelligently about the important things that concern them. Smiley wonders why Ann has gone to bed with Haydon, for in doing so she had broken "three of her own rules. Bill was Circus and he was Set—her word for family and ramifications. On either count he would be out of bounds. Thirdly, she had received him at Bywater Street, an agreed violation of territorial decencies," but however pained and puzzled Smiley is, he never asks Ann why she did so.

By the novel's end, scarred and disenchanted by both clandestine love and war, Smiley is left wondering

> whether there was any love between human beings that did not rest upon some sort of self-delusion. . . . He thought about treason and wondered whether there was mindless treason in the same way, supposedly, as there was mindless violence. It worried him that he felt so bankrupt; that whatever intellectual or philosophical precepts he clung to broke down entirely now that he was faced with the human situation.

If we feel little compassion for Smiley, remain detached from both his victories and his defeats, it is not only because of such woolly-minded lucubrations, but chiefly because le Carré has not paid proper attention to the requirements of characterization. Of Smiley's character we still know virtually nothing; of his parents and background, of his marriage and his jealousy, of why, for one instance, he and Ann have had no children. To none of these things does le Carré give a clue.

In *Smiley's People* (1980), le Carré's last novel in the saga of George Smiley, some six years have passed since the action in *Tinker, Tailor*. It is now 1978 or 1979, Smiley is seventy-two or seventy-three years old, a bit deaf in one ear, and a man who knows "his own existence too was dwindling; that he was living against the odds." Retired and writing a monograph on the seventeenth-century German poet Martin Opitz (a writer during the difficult era of the Thirty Years War when various religious and political loyalties were, as they are today, in bitter conflict), Smiley gets a telephone call from Oliver Lacon because one of Smiley's former agents, General Vladimir Miller, had been murdered on Hampstead Heath. Lacon and Sir Saul Enderby want "someone from his past. . . . Someone who can identify him, [to] damp down potential scandal. (Note how similar this is to the opening gambit in *Call for the Dead*.)

An erstwhile Red Army officer and exceptionally brave man, General Vladimir had, after his disenchantment with the Soviet system, worked underground in Moscow for the British for three years before defecting; but in the atmosphere of détente, the Intelligence Service had put him out to pasture. Pleading that a scandal might at this juncture kill the Secret Service because it still suffers the stigma of the Haydon affair, Lacon reminds Smiley, "If it does, your generation will not be least to blame. You have a duty, as we all do. A loyalty." Though Smiley is, as in the very first novel of the saga, still wondering, "Duty to what? . . . Loyalty to whom?" he reluctantly undertakes the task. Lacon wants him to say it was a mugging, but when he finds that the general was murdered by Moscow assassins, Smiley refuses and, again unofficially, launches an investigation.

Given three clues by General Vladimir—a letter from a Russian refugee in Paris named Maria Ostrakova, a single frame of film showing two naked men and women in what appears to be a brothel, and a single-line message left at the Circus headquarters for him by the general before he was murdered, saying, "Tell Max [one of Smiley's code names] that it concerns the Sandman," Smiley begins his long, lonely journey to unearth what that "it" was. With the help of his old Soviet expert, Connie Sachs, now also put out to pasture and dying, but in love with a young girl, and Toby Esterhase, another of Smiley's former intelligence colleagues dismissed from the service and now working as a salesman of phony art, Smiley gradually discovers the general's secret.

Working alone in Germany, using his old code name, *Standfast*, Smiley completes his investigation and learns that the Sandman—code name for Karla, head of Soviet Military Intelligence and Smiley's old antagonist—has a human weakness, that there is the "other Karla, Karla of the heart . . . of the one great love, the Karla flawed by humanity." Karla, it seems, was once in love with a woman—"His Ann," Connie Sachs says—and they had a daughter together. Because the woman went "Soft on the revolution. . . . Wanting the State to wither away. Asking the big 'Why?' and the big 'Why not?' " Karla had had her executed. Their daughter, Tatiana, turned out to be schizophrenic, and Karla, knowing that in the Soviet Union the treatment of mental disease was "too often complicated by political considerations," had her spirited out of the country on a false passport in the name of Maria

Ostrakova's daughter, and kept her in a Swiss asylum for treatment with funds from Soviet Intelligence. It is this act of love that Smiley decides to use to force Karla to defect.

The Lady Ann, grown older—at the very least, she must now be in her late fifties—worried by the loss of her beauty, seeks a reconciliation, which Smiley no longer wants. He cannot even bear to have her near him, both because his memories of her bring him pain—"When they made love, he knew he was the surrogate for all the men who hadn't rung [on the telephone]," and because he cannot forget Bill Haydon "whose shadow fell across her face each time he reached for her." "'Women are lawless,' [Ann] told him once, when they lay in rare peace. 'So what am I?' he had asked, and she said, 'My law.' 'So what was Haydon?' he had asked. And she laughed and said, 'My anarchy.'"

When Smiley appeals to Enderby for funds and personnel to carry out his operation, Enderby worries about the service being entrapped by the Russians, and Smiley tells him, "I'm afraid we're no longer worth the candle, Saul," but "Enderby did not care to be reminded of the limitations of British grandeur." Enderby warns Smiley that if his scheme goes awry, he will disown all of it as a "ludicrous piece of private enterprise by a senile spy who's lost his marbles." Yet, because Enderby wants Karla to use against his own politicians in Whitehall, who, full of the spirit of détente, have been crippling the Intelligence Service by cutting its funds and operational prerogatives, and also wants to trade the information they will get from Karla with the CIA "Cousins," he agrees to finance the operation. Smiley's contempt for Whitehall, for the country's leadership, is at last explicit, as is his disdain for the changing fashions in their political doctrines, each supposed to be a cure-all, but

> leaving behind it the familiar English muddle, of which, more and more in retrospect, he saw himself as a life-long moderator. He had foreborne, hoping others would forebear, and they had not. He had toiled in back rooms while shallower men held the stage. They held it still. Even five years ago he would never have admitted such sentiments. But today, peering calmly into his own heart, Smiley knew that he was unled, perhaps unleadable; that the only restraints upon him were those of his own reason, and his own humanity. As with his marriage, so with his sense of public service. I invested my life in institutions—he thought without rancour—and all I am left with is myself.

But he is not sure even of that self. Knowing he lacks Karla's absolutism about ends and means, Karla's sense that killing is a necessary and acceptable adjunct to his grand design. Smiley wonders: "'How can I win?' he asks himself; alone, restrained by doubt and a sense of decency—how can any of us—against this remorseless fusillade?" When Connie Sachs compares him to Karla, "Twin cities, we used to say you were, you and Karla, two halves of the same apple," Smiley is overwhelmed with anger, almost strikes her, because he believes that he shares neither Karla's methods nor his absolutism.

Before he puts that operation into action, Smiley goes to visit Ann at her ancestral home. "It was granite and very big, crumbling. . . . Acres of smashed greenhouses led to it; collapsed stables and an untended kitchen garden lay below in the valley." In this picture of the ruined glory of England's past, a ruined ruling class and gentry, is also the ruin of Smiley's love for Ann. Though Ann remains beautiful for him, "he didn't want her near him. . . . She kissed him on the mouth, putting her fingers along the back of his neck to guide him, and Haydon's shadow fell between them like a sword." It is a touching scene, in which their talk and its implications are almost impossible to understand, so obscure is le Carré's writing. But one thing is clear: Smiley cannot forgive Ann her betrayals, particularly the one with Haydon.

Smiley's plan against Karla is essentially blackmail. He lets Karla know that unless he comes over to the British he, Smiley, will inform Karla's Soviet masters that Karla has murdered, suborned, misappropriated public funds, all to arrange the illegal departure from the Soviet Union of his daughter by a dead mistress of "manifest anti-Soviet tendencies." Yet Smiley understands and sympathizes with Karla's concern for his daughter and admires him for having risked everything for her; put his career and his life in jeopardy in order to get her out of the Soviet Union and into that Swiss mental hospital. Smiley recognizes that his

> adversary had acquired a human face of disconcerting clarity. It was no brute whom Smiley was pursuing . . . no unqualified fanatic after all, no automaton. It was a man; and one whose downfall . . . would be caused by nothing more sinister than excessive love, a weakness with which Smiley himself . . . was eminently familiar.

For Smiley, for le Carré, lying, cheating, stealing, even killing seem, somehow, more justifiable for personal reasons, for love, than for political or ideological reasons.

All the arrangements are made; Karla is to come across at the Berlin Wall; Smiley is there, waiting, with his whole "team." Just as he sees Karla begin to walk across that no-man's-land into the West, Smiley balks. "*Don't come,* thought Smiley. *Shoot,* Smiley thought, talking to Karla's people, not his own. There was suddenly something terrible in his foreknowledge that this tiny creature was about to cut himself off from the black castle behind him." Disloyalty and defection, even Karla's, offended Smiley; and he is moved by the "one little man" he sees now before him, *one little man.* Feeling sick, Smiley perceives, "On Karla has descended the curse of Smiley's compassion; on Smiley the curse of Karla's fanaticism. I have destroyed him with the weapons I abhorred, and they are his. We have crossed each other's frontiers. We are the no-men of this no-man's land." Nonetheless, Karla does come across and they do not speak a word, but "they exchanged one more glance and perhaps each for that second did see in the other something of himself." As Karla is led away, he drops Ann's lighter, her long-ago gift to Smiley. "It lay in the halo's very edge, tilted slightly, glinting like fool's gold on the cobble. . . . [Smiley] thought of picking it up, but somehow there seemed no point."

When Karla first took that lighter from Smiley in India years before, Smiley was trying to get him to defect. Now, Smiley has succeeded in this aim, and his aide Guillam congratulates him on winning, but Smiley's reply is equivocal: "Did I? . . . Yes. Yes, well, I suppose I did." If he did, there is not much taste of victory in Smiley's mouth. In order to win, he has had to use Karla's methods and ruthlessness. In the time since Smiley has first confronted Karla, he has lost his love for Ann, so there is little point in retrieving the lighter. If Karla's wife has betrayed him politically, the Lady Ann has betrayed Smiley personally; if Smiley and Ann remain childless and thereby signal the end of their line, symbolically and literally the end of Britain's might, the last of the glories of the past, then Karla's daughter is a schizophrenic madwoman who proclaims what the Soviet state promises for the future; if Karla's ruthless absolutism is at last brought low, it is only by lowering Smiley to Karla's level in order to achieve his victory.

In the war of ideologies between the Soviet Union and the West, le Carré is saying a plague on both your houses. Appalled though he is by the flabbiness of Western liberalism, he also knows it to be superior by far to the realities of communism, nazism, and reactionary capitalism. Reflected in le Carré's novels is the shift in one segment of Western, and particularly British, public opinion from the clarity of the ideals in the hot war against the Nazis in the 1940s, from the sharpness of the anticommunist cold war against the USSR in the 1950s, to the ambiguous uncertainties of the 1960s and 1970s; in short, encapsulated in the two decades in which le Carré's novels have been published, from 1960 to 1980, we have a depiction of major social and political change. If the romantic nostalgia for the *status quo ante,* for Victorian and Edwardian solidities and certainties of a bygone England, is present in le Carré's picture of the deteriorating circumstances of British life and leadership, in the kind of individuals who are replacing the George Smileys in public life, it is combined with despair about the present and future of British institutions. As he hints in his introduction to *Philby: The Spy Who Betrayed a Generation,* le Carré very likely favors a "gentle, pragmatic form of international socialism," but neither he nor the characters of his invention find a viable political program in Britain as ruled by either Labour or the Tories.

The saga of George Smiley has come to an end in *Smiley's People,* but the ending is as equivocal as the title of the book. Who, then, are Smiley's people? What are they? Surely they are not the Whitehall politicians or the British ruling elite, any more than they are the intelligence officers of the "Circus." Instead, they are the ordinary individuals who are exploited and crushed by life, by institutions, by warring ideologies; they are the decent, the loyal, the loving, whom Smiley—and by extension le Carré—cherishes and would protect. However attractive the lure of the absolutists, their fanatic belief and ideological firmness, their justification of the means by the end, le Carré cannot surrender the worth of the ordinary "decent" individual, the ordinary decent Englishman, nor can he relinquish the inviolability of human relations to the Leviathan of the state or its purposes, be they capitalist or communist. In this, he is in the long tradition of English literature, and surely a direct descendant of George Orwell and Aldous Huxley.

HOLLY BETH KING

Child's Play in John le Carré's
Tinker, Tailor, Soldier, Spy

As a preface to his best novel, John le Carré appends the nursery rhyme: "Tinker, tailor, soldier, sailor, rich man, poor man, beggarman, thief," and the novel's title, of course, is a witty play on that rhyme. But beyond the rather facile irony of a childish rhyme attaching to a deadly serious "game" of spying and counterspying, there lies a whole intricately woven set of relationships between adults and children, between innocence and disillusionment, between loyalty and betrayal that gives the novel's title a deeper resonance. The world of George Smiley and Jim Prideaux and Bill Haydon is a world of "secret fear" where the "creak of a stair that had not creaked before; the rustle of a shutter when no wind was blowing; the car with a different number plate but the same scratch on the offside wing; the face on the Metro that you know you have seen somewhere before . . . [where] . . . any one of these [signs] was reason enough to move, change towns, identities." This world of secret fear is given an added poignancy and an added emotional dimension by being viewed—initially and then at intervals—through the eyes of children; the children, too, reveal to us the rudimentary emotions, motivations and impulses which the adults have learned to suppress, hide and deny. Often, le Carré gives us insight into his adult characters by paralleling or contrasting them to the children whose world impinges on theirs. Simultaneously, he reveals the children buried in these so deadly serious adults.

From *Clues: A Journal of Detection* 3, no. 2 (Fall/Winter 1982). © 1982 by Pat Browne.

Tinker, Tailor, Soldier, Spy tells the story of George Smiley, the unlikely hero: a "fat, podgy, and at best middle-aged" cuckold whose apparently final humiliation is to have been fired from his high level position in the British intelligence service for being allied with the wrong faction when power changed hands. With an irony obvious even to Smiley himself, his outcast status makes him the perfect candidate to investigate the suspicion that a "mole" or "deep penetration agent" has burrowed to the heart of the Circus (as the service is called in the novel) and is essentially turning it inside out, serving Moscow Centre while appearing to do the opposite. The spy's world as portrayed by le Carré is, at best, one in which paranoia is the appropriate reaction to all external signs; with the possibility of the existence of a mole, any last vestiges of stability disappear. There seems no longer any chance for security, for trust anywhere.

The novel opens in the world of children. We meet Bill Roach, a new boy at Thursgood's school: "He was a fat round child with asthma, and he spent large parts of his rest kneeling on the end of his bed, gazing through the window." Roach is the only witness to the arrival of Jim Prideaux, when the latter mysteriously joins the faculty at mid-term. At first, the innocent perspective of this lonely child seems merely to be a means for introducing us to the mysterious and opaque world of adults—and to Jim, who we later learn, has been crippled and betrayed in the last covert operation of Smiley's now dead mentor, Control. Roach very quickly takes on a variety of more complex functions in the novel, however, and establishes crucial thematic parallels that reveal the novel's basic moral context for us.

While Roach's relation to Jim is quite evident and literal, his relation to Smiley is equally important, if largely figurative and symbolic. Roach notes in his teacher and idol a loneliness which he somehow, with the intuitive acuity characteristic of him, attributes to a "great attachment that had failed him and that he longed to replace." Roach immediately attempts as he sees it—and as we begin to see it as well—to become "a stand-in replacing Jim's departed friend, whoever that friend might be." We learn much later that that departed friend was Bill Haydon, Smiley's former colleague and rival, now the real, if not the titular, head of the Circus. Jim has guessed what Smiley's researches confirm at the climax of the novel: that Bill Haydon is in fact the mole, Moscow Centre's tool at the top of the British intelligence hierarchy. With appropriate irony—perceptible only to the re-reader of the novel—Jim says to Roach when he first meets him: "Known a lot of Bills. They've all been good 'uns." Roach, with a pathetic and painful tenacity, sets out to replace this other Bill, and his loyalty and devotion serve as a stark contrast to the ultimate betrayal which Bill Haydon has committed in relation to Jim. For Haydon's betrayal is on all levels: personal, social, political, national. Jim, his best friend and perhaps his lover, has been sacrificed to Haydon's ambition or to his disillusionment.

Roach's relation to Smiley is less explicit but of equal importance in the thematic structure of the novel. At only one point, and early in the novel, does le Carré make the connection explicit. When first presenting Smiley to us, he says:

> Unlike Jim Prideaux, Mr. George Smiley was not naturally equipped for hurrying in the rain, least of all at dead of night. Indeed, he might have been the final form for which Bill Roach was the prototype. Small, podgy, and at best middle-aged, he was by appearance one of London's meek who do not inherit the earth. His legs were short, his gait anything but agile, his dress costly, ill-fitting, and extremely wet. His overcoat, which had a hint of widowhood about it, was of that black loose weave which is designed to retain moisture. Either the sleeves were too long or his arms were too short, for, as with Roach, when he wore his mackintosh, the cuffs all but concealed the fingers.

Children—primarily Bill Roach but also Jackie Lacon, the plump, awkward middle-child of one of Smiley's former associates—supply the occasional perspective through which we see the "child" buried in the adult; while the narrator never explicitly tells us Smiley's feelings, for example, the child's view superimposes that kind of perception on the more or less objective viewpoint usually given us. Smiley, as seen directly by the narrator or through the eyes of other adult characters, is controlled and cold, and le Carré is very careful not to sentimentalize him. It would certainly spoil the effect of the essentially restrained, unemotional treatment of "the great betrayal" if Smiley were to become a figure of melodrama or sentiment. Through the eyes of the child, we see a quite different man:

> a blond, good-looking man and a short fat one in an enormous overcoat like a pony blanket made their way to a sports car parked under the beech trees. For a moment she really thought there must be something wrong with the fat one, he followed so slowly and so painfully. Then, seeing the handsome man hold the car door for him, he seemed to wake, and hurried forward with a lumpy skip. Unaccountably, this gesture upset her afresh. A storm of sorrow seized her and her mother could not console her.

More importantly, the treatment of Bill Roach, who in some ways is a young Smiley, comes to function as a key to our understanding of the hero, as a means of filling in the blanks about his past, his character, his feelings. Smiley, by the time we meet him, has learned to suppress himself, so that even the narrative which gives us his point of view, cannot really tell us all of what Smiley doesn't allow himself to feel. The dispossessed Roach is the product of a broken home. Like Smiley, he is naturally humble, blaming himself for his many shortcomings; more important, he takes responsibility for everything, most especially "the break-up of his parents' marriage, which he should have seen coming and taken steps to prevent." Smiley likewise takes the weight of the world on his shoulders, and is criticized for his overconcern for Jackie Lacon when she tumbles from her pony. Lacon says to him, "You're not responsible for everyone, you know, George."

In a parody of the adult world of spies, cover, disguises and betrayal, Roach becomes a "spy," first in the figurative sense of being someone who keeps his eyes open. Later, Jim enlists his aid in "watching" for the unaccounted-for stranger, for the mysterious pursuer, or for any signs that Jim is still being followed after his failed mission and his crippling. It is Roach's loneliness, his timidity, his status as outcast that makes him "a natural watcher"; it is his character which reveals to us Smiley's psychology and motivation. Spies do not become lonely men; it is lonely men who become spies. As Roach's one true devotion and attachment is to Jim (a condemnatory contrast to Haydon), so Smiley's one attachment and perhaps his "last illusion of an illusionless man" is his love for his wayward wife, Ann. That love, which Haydon—and his Russian Svengali, Karla—use against Smiley as his one "weakness," is paradoxically what saves Smiley for us, what preserves him as a hero in a world of ultimate betrayal. Smiley remains tenaciously and perhaps foolishly faithful to something—not to an idea, but to an individual. For Smiley, his is a trade where there is only the "negative vision," where the "political generality was meaningless," where only "the particular in life" had value. Haydon, on the other hand, has betrayed everything:

> Haydon had betrayed. As a lover, a colleague, a friend; as a patriot; as a member of that inestimable body that Ann loosely called the Set; in every capacity, Haydon had overtly pursued one aim and secretly achieved its opposite. Smiley knew very well that even now he did not grasp the scope of that appalling duplicity.

The child's world is scarcely more innocent or idyllic. What we see through Roach's experience is only a more simplified version of the same things: loneliness, fear, guilt and loss and pain—salvaged only by a kind of thoughtless and selfless devotion. In an ironic reversal of the precocious suffering of Bill Roach, we see the figures of adults who have never truly grown up. This reversal is reflected first of all in the use in spying terminology of the language of childhood. The school for training agents is called "the Nursery"; Control's secretaries are called "Mothers"; the intelligence establishment is called "the Circus"; bodyguards are called "babysitters." The lies, the disguises, the pretense resemble vaguely a child's make-believe world, and certainly the secret service in modern day Britain is more full of sound and fury than of any solid importance. That fact is Haydon's apparent reason for collaborating with the Russians: the game in Britain is ultimately of no significance and he has larger designs for himself.

Peter Guillam, erstwhile associate and "friend" of Smiley's and one who aids Smiley in ferreting out the mole, is an almost forty-year-old man who is still somehow a boy. As one of the other characters perceives him:

> And young Guillam needs a holiday, thought Mendel. He'd seen *that* happen before, too: the tough ones who crack at forty. They lock it away, pretend it isn't there, lean on grown-ups who turn out not to be so grown up after all; then one day it's all over them, and their heroes come tumbling down and they're sitting at their desks with the tears pouring onto the blotter.

When Haydon's treachery is finally unmasked, Smiley thinks of Guillam: "He worried, in a quite paternal way, about Guillam, and wondered how he would take the late strains of growing up." For Peter, Haydon has been a combination idol and father-figure, and his growing up is having ultimately to surrender that image—accepting the necessary disillusionment and going beyond it. His maturity comes when after feeling "orphaned" he essentially forgives Haydon.

Perhaps the most important example of the child-adult link is the ironic parallel that Jim Prideaux makes between Bill Roach and Haydon, his other Bill. It is between the child who attempts to love and protect his friend by reaching out of the limits and limitations of his child's world, and the adult who betrays everyone and everything because he has finally been unwilling to grow up. Roach, who tries to be a "stand-in" for Jim's missing or lost friend, though he doesn't understand how adults "love each other," dedicates his life to the protection of Jim. Haydon, on the other hand, betrays all the loyalties, all the promises, all the values he supposedly stands for—the final and most damning of all being the betrayal of Jim, his friend and perhaps his lover. As Haydon describes them in an early letter: "He's my other half; between us we'd make one marvelous man."

Haydon's ironical "boyishness" becomes, on the contrary, more sinister as we see the significance of its context. Early in the novel, while Smiley is just beginning to unravel the complex past—his and the Circus's—which will reveal the identity of the mole, he goes to visit Connie Sachs, formerly a Circus employee and victim of the same "housecleaning" which cost Smiley his position. As he taps her memory, she begins to reminisce about the old days, the days of glory of Smiley and his generation. She remembers the now middle-aged men as "lovely, lovely boys," of whom Haydon was the most "golden." But while Smiley seems to settle into middle age with a vengeance, Haydon somehow manages to maintain a kind of schoolboy quality to the very end. When he first appears in the novel, Peter Guillam sees him first as "strangely black and tall," then later as "handsome and absurdly young"; Smiley remembers him at the Circus as "favourite boy." And Haydon some-how never escaped that youth of his which held so much promise, that promise which Connie referred to and which Smiley remembers:

> Connie's lament rang in his ears: "Poor loves. Trained to Empire, trained to rule the waves. . . . You're the last, George, you and Bill." He saw with painful clarity an ambitious man born to the big canvas, brought up to rule, divide and conquer, whose visions and vanities all were fixed . . . upon the world's game; for whom the reality was a poor island with scarcely a voice that would carry across the water.

So it is through the eyes and the images of children, finally, that the moral center of the novel is revealed. In the world of le Carré's novels, where the key to survival is "an infinite capacity for suspicion," love for and com-mitment to another human being is paradoxically the ultimate salvation. Both Roach's love for Jim and Smiley's for Ann are in some ways blind, foolish, incomplete. And that love rests hardly at all upon the ultimate worth of the loved one or the quality or completeness of the relationship. Roach perceives and suffers for Jim's pain and loss without understanding it; Smiley continues to love Ann even though she often mystifies him and even though her infi-delities give him much pain. But this love and commitment must somehow transcend reason, rationality, the "objective value" of the loved object. Bill Haydon has plenty of "reasons" for his actions; and in most circumstances, we must acknowledge along with Smiley that neither the service, nor the political establishment, nor the economic system, corrupt and self-serving as they all are, "deserve" loyalty in any objective sense of the word. That assumption underlies, in fact, the mood of bleakness and despair which is so much a part of the world of le Carré's novels. Both Roach and Smiley take responsibility for other human beings, even when that responsibility seems futile. Before the final revelation of Haydon's treachery, Smiley thinks of all this:

> He had no sense of conquest that he knew of. His thoughts, as often when he was afraid, concerned people. He had no theories or judgments in particular. He simply wondered how everyone would be affected; and he felt responsible. He thought of Jim and Sam and Max and Connie and Jerry Westerby, and personal loyalties all broken; in a separate category he thought of Ann and the hopeless dislocation of their talk on the Cornish cliffs; he wondered whether there was any love between human beings that did not rest upon some sort of self-delusion; he wished he could just get up and walk out before it happened, but he couldn't. . . . It worried him that he felt so bankrupt; that whatever intellectual or philosophical precepts he clung to broke down entirely now that he was faced with the human situation.

The love which Smiley wonders about, a love that does not rest upon self-delusion, is the love of the child: thoughtless, irrational, and loyal. The children in the novel, and the child in Smiley, offer the only fragile hope there is in the world of *Tinker, Tailor, Soldier, Spy*.

HELEN S. GARSON

Enter George Smiley:
Le Carré's Call for the Dead

George Smiley, a unique kind of spy, makes his initial appearance, center stage, in John le Carré's first book, *Call for the Dead,* 1962. It is Smiley who figures prominently in most of the author's subsequent work, concluding with the recently published, highly successful novel, *Smiley's People.* Either in the foreground or background, Smiley turns up in seven of the nine le Carré books, the character that provides the link from one work to the next.

Like the great detectives of the latter part of the nineteenth century and of the golden age of mystery novels in the twentieth century, Smiley is a memorable, remarkable person. However, his qualities are not theirs. He does not resemble the greatest of the great detectives, Holmes, in breadth of erudition, nor Poirot in brilliance, nor Lord Peter Wimsey in idiosyncracies. Neither is he handsome nor dashing. He stands apart from famous spies of fiction and in no way suggests his contemporary, James Bond, the eternally young, athletic, superhuman hero who is a frequently copied model for spy fiction.

If Smiley strikes any note of recognition in the modern reader, it is in his affinity, in various ways, to the antihero, nonhero, or new hero of twentieth-century fiction.

Containing characteristics of the traditional, familiar hero and those of the contemporary antihero, Smiley is the prince forever imprisoned inside

From *Clues: A Journal of Detection* 3, no. 2 (Fall/Winter 1982). © 1982 by Pat Browne.

the frog. He does battle for a tarnished cause, not in sunlight on ski slopes or sparkling ocean, but on dreary London streets or shabby down-at-the-heels houses. We see him in darkness and in rain. No romantic, moon-filled love scenes exist for Smiley, only sleepless, lonely nights.

His support system, when there is one, consists of other solitary men, whose personal lives must always be subordinate to the work. Few have wives and children. Like Smiley, most seem to be orphans with no past to encumber them. All live in a present struggle and fear; and the future offers little hope.

With victories that are limited and partial, Smiley is always left not with the sparkling trophy cup of the hero but with the taste of wormwood. Smiley does not save all of the Western world from destruction, not even England. He can only plug a small hole in the dike that is eroding from within and without. In the constant, often inept struggle of the Secret Service to keep the beleaguered bulwark of democracy from falling into the vast sea of communism, Smiley is used and misused, shelved and recalled to duty more than once. His life is as much a fight against the politically powerful, self-aggrandizing men in his own government as is his deadly combat with the enemy.

Call for the Dead lays the structure that successive books build on: England after World War II, a battered country, struggling to rebuild and to retain its independence not only against foes but also rich, tough friends. Yet, le Carré makes it clear, England is not a land of heroes. Mediocre people run things, more careful of themselves than of the nation. While the enemy grows in wealth and power, the British flounder. Corruption more wide-spread than ever before threatens the fabric of society, a point scarcely visible in this first book, but ever more significant as the author develops his philo-sophic views in works that become increasingly complex over the next two decades.

Although the novelist provides deeper insights into his political judg-ments as he continues to write, in this introductory novel le Carré tells more about Smiley than he is to do in successive novels. In the six other novels in which Smiley appears, le Carré fleshes out his character and personality. But a reader coming to the later books first finds bits and pieces that may prove tantalizing without the earlier information, and he may need to search out the beginning works for greater understanding. Clearly, le Carré considers it vital for us to know Smiley. In *Call for the Dead,* it is the most important relationship established, and le Carré signals that by entitling his opening chapter "A Brief History of George Smiley."

Immediately we are plunged into the protagonist's life. We learn of Smiley's disastrous marriage to Lady Ann Sercomb. His love for Ann is and will always remain Smiley's greatest vulnerability. Because of her he has a wound that never heals. Ann is Smiley's hostage to fortune. Middle-aged when he marries her at the end of World War II, a man "always withdrawn" and one whose intelligence work had forced him to avoid "the temptations of friendship and human loyalty," Smiley hopes to find with Ann a new life, one that he has dreamed about. He seeks the quiet life of a scholar at Oxford, the peace and pleasure of vacations in Cornwall, his beautiful wife by his side.

All things intervene. The world's hope for peace at the end of the hostilities turns into the Cold War that still prevails today. Because of that, Smiley's regression into the delights of seventeenth-century German poetry comes to an end after only two years. In spite of his earlier longing for the academic milieu, when he is recalled to the Service he returns with some relish, for his personal life has come apart. His wife, Ann, has gone off with a Cuban racing driver, an act which leaves Smiley like "lost luggage . . . unclaimed." And although "a little of George Smiley . . . died," with the betrayal and the divorce, he is ready to take up intelligence work again.

Leaving behind his dream of order and contentment, he returns to London, a city which is to be his home in all subsequent novels. However, in *A Murder of Quality,* which follows immediately after *Call for the Dead,* Smiley, cast in the role of detective, goes back to Oxford as visitor and investigator. In fact the only real value of this minor piece is that it provides more of a milieu, a place (now a place lost), for Smiley. The Oxford environment, its history, its dons, its politics, become important in the later novels, as le Carré attempts to understand both treason and loyalty and the ways in which certain men choose their destinies.

In *Call for the Dead* Oxford is referred to but not seen. Smiley, the former Oxford student, has only a taste of retirement and the prosaic life before reentering the Service.

Smiley's hiatus has been brief, but nevertheless during that time the structure and character of the intelligence service have changed. His friends are gone, some dead, some seeking other kinds of work, or, as in the case of the former chairman, Steed-Asprey, searching for "another civilisation." The Service, once an agency run by a few exceptionally able "amateurs," has become an efficient but intrigue-ridden bureaucracy presided over by an empire builder named Maston.

Maston is the new kind of bureaucrat, the man who knows how to move papers, to please cabinet members, to change positions like clothing, according to the political weather. Popular with his ministers, he is scorned by those who work with him. Known officially as "the Minister's Adviser on Intelligence," he has also been labelled "the Head Eunuch" by the former chairman, and nicknamed "Marlene Dietrich" by the CID. He is described even more devastatingly by le Carré as "a cloak and dagger man," one who wears "the cloak for his masters," and who saves "the dagger for his servants."

This is the man for whom Smiley works and who has sent for him as the story gets underway.

In the middle of the night Maston meets with Smiley at the office at Oxford Circus to discuss the death of a Foreign Office employee named Fennan, whom Smiley had interviewed two days earlier. Deeply disturbed, though pretending great calm, Maston informs Smiley that Fennan committed suicide after sending a note to the Foreign Secretary accusing Smiley of questioning his loyalty and ruining his career.

Smiley finds the situation unbelievable, because the interview with Fennan had been ordinary and insignificant. When the Director of Security had received an unsigned letter claiming that Fennan had once been a member of the Communist Party while a student at Oxford, the Director sent Smiley to check on Fennan.

Smiley describes for Maston the meeting with Fennan as one incongruent with suicide. He met with Fennan in a busy office, walked with him in the park, drank coffee in an expresso bar. After Fennan talked about his early years, Smiley assured him that there was nothing to worry about, that there was no reason for the Department to take any action against him.

But Fennan is dead and there is the damaging letter to the Foreign Secretary. Maston, less interested in truth than in finding a way to smooth over the consequences, expects Smiley to cooperate fully in protecting the Department, an act which really means protecting Maston. Exerting subtle pressure on Smiley to provide a way out of the situation, Maston lets him know he is expendable. That view remains prevalent throughout the book, even after it becomes clear that Smiley's sense about Fennan was correct, that he was not a potential suicide when Smiley interviewed him.

In spite of the awkwardness, even the indelicacy of the situation, Maston insists that Smiley must be the one to see the widow, to learn as much as possible about Fennan and the reasons for his action. With that decision Maston ignites the spark that sets off one incident after another in a chain reaction of violence and death. Had Maston understood Smiley, his character, his intelligence, his tenacity, he would not have insisted that Smiley be the one to put the case together. He miscalculates, however, and Smiley does not provide him with the easy out he wants. Instead, Smiley presents a strong suspicion of murder, and when Maston refuses to support him he tenders a letter of resignation.

Resignation from the Service, though, does not alter Smiley's decision to pursue the Fennan matter to an honorable conclusion. A surprising phone call at Fennan's house, a letter sent to Smiley's office by Fennan, setting up a lunch date for the afternoon following his death, and a stranger with a gun waiting for Smiley in his home all convince him of the likelihood of Fennan's murder and the possibility of his own. Even if Smiley wished to forget all about Fennan he cannot, for he himself has become a target for the killer as a result of his investigation.

Unable to call directly on his agency for help once he resigns, Smiley enlists the aid of Inspector Mendel whom he met at the time of Fennan's death and shortly before Mendel's retirement from Scotland Yard. Mendel, a figure le Carré uses again in later books, becomes Smiley's ally, the one he turns to for assistance in running down the murderer. The Inspector is more than an assistant in crime solving; he befriends Smiley in every way possible, sheltering him in his home when there is danger, carrying on when Smiley lies dangerously ill in the hospital, the result of an attack on his life, calling on resources available to him through police work, and setting up a liaison between the hospitalized Smiley and Peter Guillam, a colleague at the Ministry of Defense.

Guillam, another le Carré favorite who appears in future novels, is a specialist in "satellite espionage," clever, sophisticated, extremely competent, a man "who always has a timetable and a penknife." Taste and culture mark Guillam, like Smiley, like the former Chairman of the Service, Steed-Asprey: Smiley, the German scholar; Guillam, who gave Smiley and Ann a Watteau sketch for a wedding gift; Steed-Asprey, who bought them a group of Dresden figurines. These marks of cultivation distinguish symbolically the kind of leaders England once had and is now in danger of losing to the philistines, the Mastons, the bureaucrats who possess veneer and no substance, who buy "off the peg" because they have no recognition of intrinsic worth.

With the combination of the police work of Mendel, the espionage expertise of Guillam, and the mixture of instinctive/deductive powers of Smiley, they are able to connect the death of Fennan to a communist group called "the East German Steel Mission." When that happens, the story, tautly suspenseful even in its quiet beginning, intensifies as the deadly game of hunter and hunted is played out.

Much of le Carré's uniqueness as spy writer lies in his wide range of vision. Nothing in his work, from this novel to his most recent, ever divides world politics into black and white, good and bad. The East Germans, an enemy in this and other books, have their reasons—valid for them, though destructive for the West—and the thinking person must understand, even admire the courage, passion and the dedication behind their actions. Thus, it is with sorrow that Smiley, representing le Carré's view, struggles against a force he cannot hate. He knows all too well the terrible past which brought many dedicated men into the socialist and ultimately the communist orbit.

During the rise of Nazism, the era of the thirties, Smiley had been sent by the Service to Germany, following a period in South America and Central Europe where he got his initial training. Though ostensibly a lecturer at a German University, his real mission, undercover, was to find potential agents to work for British intelligence. Before the fighting began, Smiley did none of the actual recruiting, but in 1939 he was given more active and dangerous assignments. He personally set up a network of German agents; to do this he worked as a Swedish manufacturer's representative in small-arms sales, traveling from Sweden to Switzerland and Germany. During the four years that Smiley stayed in that job the network expanded successfully and con-tinued until 1945, the end of the war, although Smiley returned home two years earlier, in 1943. With the cessation of hostilities most of the agents dispersed, but a few remained, and willingly or reluctantly were caught up in the Russian web when Germany was divided into two zones.

The strength of the ties that are created among people whose fate and lives depend on one another can never be measured. In wartime the allegiance that one human being has to another is tested by political loyalties and obligations. For the espionage agent the choice is particularly cruel, because situations change: countries that are allies in one war may be enemies in the next or in an uneasy peace. Russia, Britain's former ally, has become the foe in a war of nerves that has global dimensions. With East Germany as a satellite, the Russians are able to manipulate events so that they appear blameless for hostile activities of the East Germans. Ironically, because the English do not recognize East Germany as a nation, any dealings they have with that sector must be conducted vis-à-vis the Russians. For the average Briton, a more repugnant outcome of World War II is the rebuilding and rearming of West Germany by America and England. In the universal game of chess, individuals serve as pawns; they are dispensable, a fact nobody recognizes more keenly than Smiley.

Call for the Dead, as well as certain other le Carré novels, has former teammates pitted against each other in a battle to the death. Each knows, respects and cares about the other, perhaps even to the point of sacrificing his own life at the ultimate moment of confrontation. Smiley, who is called by his former colleague—now his enemy—"the best he'd ever met," wins a barren victory. In the delirium of illness following the death of the man who was once his comrade, he cries out in telling lines from *The Duchess of Malfi*: "I bad thee, when I was distracted of my wits, go kill my dearest friend, and thou has done it."

That friend, in another world and another time, was one who "dreamed of peace and freedom." He was "mercurial, absolute, and had fought to build a civilisation," but was defeated by the "rationalistic, protective" Smiley. Before that moment comes, Peter Guillam has a vision of the German spy as "a living component of all our romantic dreams, he stood at the mast with Conrad, sought the lost Greece with Byron." Yet the man who was the dreamer, the voyager, followed the path to the monolith. For Smiley, then, there is no other choice but to destroy him.

Sick at heart, Smiley considers himself the lesser man. His grief in the killing makes one think of Othello's words as he contemplates the death of Desdemona: "It is the cause, it is the cause, my soul."

The cause is the survival of the remnants of Western democracy. There is little left and the hour is late. Still, Smiley never questions the basic issues. He, as le Carré's spokesman, sees fundamental differences between the two systems and believes that there must be a struggle unto death to save what can be saved. Although le Carré has few illusions about twentieth-century politics, he has not gone the way of Graham Greene, whom he admires greatly, who finds modern democracy as dreadful, terrifying and corrupt as communism.

Smiley gains few satisfactions from the conclusion of the Fennan investigation. Questions remain unanswered and the entire truth will never be known even to Smiley. Although it is finally clear that Fennan could not have committed suicide, larger issues are not settled, particularly his role or lack of one in the spy network. The central figures are dead, leaving Smiley with suppositions and a longing to understand the meanings behind the grim events. He is never satisfied with the appearance of victory. He wants to look into the human heart, but that is always denied him.

Beneath the veneer of the calm rationalist is one who feels the pain of the displaced, the scorned, the betrayed. Having lived close to "intolerance gone mad" in Germany, he has great sympathy for the Jews, all of them, those who died and those who survived the Holocaust of Europe, and those who live in the free nations, putting up with being treated always as outsiders, suffering the veiled anti-Semitism of the Establishment, a different type of cold war. Smiley understands why an Englishman like Fennan, a Jew, flirted in his youth with communism as "an outlet for his anger and revulsion" against the spreading fascist ideology. Even when Mrs. Fennan, a Holocaust victim, furiously rejects Smiley's gentle pity, he feels compassion for her. More than that, he recognizes in his solicitude that some people are like delicate Dresden porcelain. Broken, they may be mended, but irreparable damage remains.

The gentleness at the core of Smiley's being makes us care for him. We are as concerned for his unhappiness as he is for others that have been injured. However, we have the comfort of being able to trust him implicitly, whereas he must be wary. Feelings can betray him, cause him to make wrong judgments, even fatal ones; and he has to test, probe, watch and analyze constantly. His ability to do these things protects his life, if not his emotions. In his work, ever watchful, containing responses that might undermine his position, he exercises caution. However, to drive out emotions completely would be to give up a great part of himself. Thus, in private ways, George Smiley will be buffeted by his passions—secret, concealed but always there—for all of his life.

In his personal world he is and will remain vulnerable. He is open to a fatal blow at any time, a man deceived, cuckolded, and deserted by his wife; yet, when Ann calls him back to her, he goes, recognizing sadly his own "pathetic quest for love." Although knowing now that Ann is incapable of fidelity, that his future is uncertain and inscrutable, Smiley chooses to live with passion and pain rather than emptiness and calm. He will struggle always, futilely and perhaps unknowingly, to be admitted to the magic kingdom, where the kiss of the Princess would transform and free him from the dark forest of his existence.

GLENN W. MOST

The Hippocratic Smile:
John le Carré and the Traditions
of the Detective Novel

*Under her left breast and tight against the flame-colored shirt lay the
silver handle of a knife I had seen before. The handle was in the shape
of a naked woman. The eyes of Miss Dolores Gonzales were half-open
and on her lips there was the dim ghost of a provocative smile.*

*"The Hippocrates smile," the ambulance intern said, and sighed.
"On her it looks good."*

—RAYMOND CHANDLER, *The Little Sister*

The true mystery in a mystery novel is not that of the crime committed
near its beginning and solved near its end but instead that posed by the
nature of the detective who solves it. To be sure, the crime is always puzzling,
either because it is so bizarre or because it seems so simple, and the plot of
the novel always moves from the absence of an answer for this puzzle,
through a series of false answers, to a final and therefore presumably true
one. But at the end, there always is that final answer, that solution which
accounts both for the initial crime and for the various inadequate hypotheses
to which it gave rise; and, at the end, the reader wonders why he had not
seen the answer sooner. For the mystery of the crime is, in essence, simply
a riddle, a question that seems obscure before it is answered but oddly simple
afterwards, a puzzle for which there is always allegedly one and only one
solution. Its difficulty derives from the fact that a truth has been *concealed,*

From *The Poetics of Murder: Detective Fiction and Literary Theory,* edited by
Glenn W. Most and William W. Stowe. © 1983 by Glenn W. Most and William W.
Stowe. Harcourt Brace Jovanovich, 1983.

its ease from the fact that a *truth* has been concealed. For no concealment can be flawless (the fruitlessness of the genre's eternal search for the perfect crime is enough to show this), and the very measures that are taken to disguise the crime are the ones that in the end will point unmistakably toward its perpetrator. If one reason for the mystery novel's conventional preference for the crime of murder is that murder is perhaps the only human action in which there are usually only two participants, one absolutely incapable of narrating it later and the other disinclined to do so, then we may be tempted to explain this as part of an effort to make the puzzle as hard to solve as possible; yet the victim's unwilling silence is always more then compensated for by the murderer's onerous knowledge. The certainty of the latter's correct awareness of what really happened is the fixed point around which the novel moves and to which it can and therefore must inevitably return. The victim may have been duped by the murderer; but in the end, it is always the murderer who is the greater dupe: for he had imagined that merely concealing an answer would suffice to make it irretrievable, and had not realized that any process of concealment can be reversed and become, step by step, a process of discovery. The victim, whose corpse abashed survivors surround, may seem lonely in his death—but the criminal, to whom finally all point their fingers and proclaim, "Thou art the man," is, in fact, in his utter nakedness, far more terrifyingly so.

But if the crime is, in essence, merely a puzzle, the detective who solves it is himself a figure of far deeper and more authentic mystery. All the other characters may be stereotypes and may turn out to have acted from the most banal of motives; but the detective fits into none of the categories with which the actions of all the others can be exhaustively explained, and his own motives are cloaked in an obscurity that is never finally lifted. He is fundamentally at odds with the society of which all the other characters are part; he is the bearer of true rationality, opposed to both the murderer (who degrades reason to the cleverness with which an irrational crime can never be adequately concealed) and the police (who represent a reason that is institutionalized, technocratic, and therefore quite futile); he is the figure of decency surrounded by selfishness and immorality, the sole searcher for truth in a world given over to delusion and duplicity. He is in every regard a marginal figure: his profession is not to have a profession but to investigate all those who do; he derives his income not from a steady and productive job but, case by case, from those who have such jobs but require his services; he alone can move, competently but never at home, through every stratum of society, from the mansions from which the poor are excluded to the slums that the wealthy abhor; he is almost always single or divorced (it is marriage that provides the most fertile soil for this genre's crimes); his parents are almost never mentioned, and he is invariably childless. It is his freedom from all such categories that permits him so clearly to see through their workings in all the other characters; but at the same time this dispensation from the rules that bind all others makes him an enigma without an answer, a mystery which is never solved. What does the detective do between cases?

Poe, with his usual prescience, endowed the literary detective with this aura of mystery at his birth. The first sentence of the first mystery story, "The Murders in the Rue Morgue," points the paradox nicely: "The mental features discoursed of as the analytical, are, in themselves, but little susceptible of analysis." What is this analytical power to whose description Poe devotes the first pages of the story? His analysis of it juggles paradoxes of appearance and reality, means and ends, method and intuition, without even pretending seriously to provide a satisfactory answer. We are told that the man who possesses this power "is fond of enigmas, of conundrums, hieroglyphics"; but the power itself (which suffices to solve such trivial problems, though they may confound us) cannot be approached directly, but only through the detour of such examples as checkers and whist provide. Even Poe's final correlation of ingenuity with fancy and the analytical ability with imagination serves only to translate the dilemma into the terms of English Romantic literary theory, not to resolve it. From the beginning, that is, Poe is at pains to show us that the mysteries that can be solved are not as mysterious as those posed by the power that solves them; and his method is to use answerable puzzles as a means of demonstrating the unanswerableness of the deeper puzzle of the power that can answer them. The celebrated anecdotes that follow this opening—Dupin guesses the narrator's thoughts and solves the double murder in the Rue Morgue—are introduced simply as being "somewhat in the light of a commentary upon the propositions just advanced," and even they do not answer the questions that opening raises. They provide further, more extended examples; they pretend to demonstrate by narrative rather than by analogy; but they multiply the enigma rather than resolve it. Hence, not the least of the red herrings in Poe's story is its very form: by its structure it seems to begin with a mystery (what is the analytical power?) and then to provide its solution (by the narrative of Dupin's exploits). But those exploits—by their bizarre mixture of reckless leaps to conclusions with scrupulously logical method, by their combination of erratic erudition and cheap theatricality, and above all by their wildly improbable success—serve only to deepen the mystery rather than to dispel it. We ought to have been warned by the very name Dupin (which does not quite conceal the French verb meaning "to dupe")—or by the epigraph from

Sir Thomas Browne that Poe brazenly affixes to his story and that propounds
the solubility of questions to which no answer could possibly be found:
"What song the Syrens sang, or what name Achilles assumed when he hid
himself among women, although puzzling questions, are not beyond *all* conjecture."

Hence, the mystery of who killed Madam l'Espanaye and her daughter
is definitively, if oddly, resolved; but the mystery of Dupin never is. The
details of his past are entirely obscure; of his income we learn only that it
suffices to free him of any occupation other than reading, writing, and talking all night long; we do not even know what he looks like. Dupin is, of
course, an extreme example; but in the way in which he penetrates all others'
secrets while remaining opaque to us he provides the model for all his followers:

> He boasted to me, with a low chuckling laugh, that most men,
> in respect to himself, wore windows in their bosoms, and was
> wont to follow up such assertions by direct and very startling
> proofs of his intimate knowledge of my own. His manner at these
> moments was frigid and abstract; his eyes were vacant in expres-
> sion; while his voice, usually a rich tenor, rose into a treble which
> would have sounded petulant but for the deliberateness and entire
> distinctness of the enunciation.

The vacancy of his eyes seals him against our inspection: as the oracle, filled
with divine inspiration, of which this latter sentence is designed to remind
us, he offers us troubling insights into the truths we conceal within us, but
himself escapes our detection.

Such coyness is, of course, profoundly seductive; and, from Poe onwards, the mystery genre has fascinated its readers at least as much through
the person of its detective as through the ingenuity of its puzzles or the
exoticism of its crimes. Future historians of the genre could do worse than
to point to the striking proximity, in place and time, of the rise of the
detective story and of that of the modern biography: for detective stories are,
for many readers, installments in the fragmentary biographies of their heroes,
each displaying his familiar virtues under a new and surprising light. Every
new case presents a challenge to the detective's skills: we know he will meet
it, and are pleased to discover we had not foreseen how. The natural result
is the cult of the literary detective, so familiar in our time, whether that cult
is centered upon holy sites (like number 221B, Baker Street) or upon the
gifted actor who has succeeded in incarnating the detective on film (like
Bogart's Sam Spade or Philip Marlowe).

But if the detective's essential enigmatic quality has persisted now for almost a century and a half, the specific form it has assumed has undergone radical transformation during that time. For the sake of simplicity (and at the cost of a certain schematism), we may distinguish between two basic and largely successive traditions: one that may be called English (though it begins with Poe) because it is brought to its classic form by Arthur Conan Doyle and continued by other British authors like Agatha Christie; and another, primarily American tradition, founded by Dashiell Hammett, perfected by Raymond Chandler, and prolonged by Ross Macdonald.

In the English tradition, every effort is made to keep the detective free of any other participation in the case he is investigating than that necessarily involved in his solution of its perplexities. This is, indeed, one of the hallmarks of the early modern detective story that separates it decisively from such forerunners as *Oedipus the King* or *Hamlet,* in which the investigator is intimately bound up, by links at least familial and dynastic, with the case in question. The invention of the professional detective, who investigates not because anything is at stake for him (other than the discovery of the truth) but simply because that is his job, serves the purpose of keeping him free of any taint of complicity in the case. In this way, investigation and event, thought, and object, are kept entirely distinct from one another. The separation between these two realms engenders a narrative that can begin with the widest possible distance between them and moves, more or less haltingly, toward their identification. The standard plot within this tradition begins with the discovery of the crime in its apparently absolute inexplicability. The detective is brought into the case either by the accidental circumstance of his proximity or by a client who has been unjustly accused and whose innocence he is required to establish. The detective then begins to investigate, by means of perception (the discovery of clues), discourse (the interviewing of various parties), and the logically self-consistent interpretation of the material he thereby acquires. His activity proceeds until the mental construct of the original crime he has been gradually refining finally coincides with that crime: at this point there is at last an exact correspondence between his thought and the real event that had occurred before his entrance onto the scene, the discrepancies that had provided the impetus to his revision of earlier hypotheses have been resolved, and the truth can be announced. The criminal confesses and the innocent suspect is redeemed; the police enter and the detective exits; justice is done. In such plots, two particularly noteworthy kinds of exclusions tend to operate. On the level of the individual characters, relations of sex or violence between the detective and the other figures tend to be prohibited: the detective neither experiences nor exerts sexual attraction, and he neither inflicts nor is seriously endangered by physical violence. On the level of society, the characters tend to be isolated during the investigation from forces that would otherwise interfere with it; the result is a certain unity of place, which, at the limit, secludes all the possible suspects in a train, a hotel, or an island.

In all these regards, the contrast posed by the American tradition could hardly be more striking. Consider the plot structure most frequently found among these latter authors. The novel begins, not with a murder, but with the client's hiring the detective in some far more minor matter: a painting has been stolen, a blackmailer must be foiled, a runaway teenager must be found. The detective begins to investigate: and only then do the murders begin. The detective relentlessly pursues his course on a path increasingly strewn with corpses until a truth is uncovered for which the original assignment represented at best a misunderstanding, at worst a ploy. It generally turns out at the end either that the client was himself the criminal and had attempted to lure the detective into becoming the unwitting accomplice of his designs or that the minor incident that had brought the detective onto the scene was merely a distant epiphenomenon of a deeply hidden, far more heinous crime, which cannot remain unresolved if that minor incident is to be adequately explained. Here the detective is not only the solution, he is also part of the problem, the catalyst who by his very introduction both provokes murders and solves them. In the figure of this investigator, the investigation and its object become inextricably intertwined. Correspondingly, the two exclusions we noted in the English tradition tend to be annulled. On the one hand, the detective's relations with other characters are free from neither sex nor violence: he feels acutely a disturbing erotic interest in the women of the case, which they are all too ready to exploit; and conversely, he can become the victim of considerable violence and be seriously threatened with death, just as he can employ methods of interrogation and coercion that the English novelists might dismiss as ungentlemanly. These features are not just sensationalistic but are designed to further implicate the detective in the case and to jeopardize his autonomy: a sexual involvement would abolish his status as outsider, whereas the scenes of violence turn him into a version of the victim or of the murderer. And on the other hand, the ever-widening circle of his investigation constantly draws in new characters and forces that might seem to hinder his initial task but, in fact, fulfill it by placing it in its full context: it is only by indirections that he finds directions out, and his travels through the extreme reaches of different social classes and different parts of the city, always in pursuit of a unified truth, link what

might have seemed disparate and unconnected fragments into a complex and
deeply corrupt social network.

It is tempting to accuse the English tradition of naiveté and its products
of being sterile intellectual puzzles or to praise the American tradition for its
sophistication and social realism. But this is shortsighted. Not only can the
English authors produce plots of a deeply satisfying complexity and psychological richness; not only can the American novelists fall into the trap of
identifying the bizarre or the sordid with the realistic and fail to recognize
how stereotyped their own plots are. More importantly, both traditions provide valid, if competing, versions of the fundamental mystery of the detective
without which the genre can scarcely be conceived. In both, the detective is,
in fact, the figure for the reader within the text, the one character whose
activities most closely parallel the reader's own, in object (both reader and
detective seek to unravel the mystery of the crime), in duration (both are
engaged in the story from the beginning, and when the detective reveals his
solution the reader can no longer evade it himself and the novel can end),
and in method (a tissue of guesswork and memory, of suspicion and logic).
That is why the literary detective (as distinguished, one supposes, from the
real-life one) tends so strongly to marginality, for he is quite literally the only
character who resides at and thereby defines the margin between text and
reader, facing inward to the other characters in the story and facing outward
to the reader with whom only he is in contact; so, too, that is why he is so
isolated, insulated from family, economy, and his own past, for all such
factors as these tend to be suppressed as distractions by readers during the
activity of reading any literary text. To be sure, in cases where the story is
told not by the detective himself or by an omniscient narrator but instead
by the detective's confidante, the reader's identification may be split between
the Holmes figure and the Watson one: but here the Watson character provides one pole of convenient stupidity that the reader is proud to avoid
(though he must exert himself to do so), whereas the Holmes one represents
the ideal pole of perfect knowledge, of an entirely correct reading, toward
which the reader aims and which he ought never quite to be able to attain.
In other regards as well (the suspense of the delay that intervenes between
desire and fulfillment or between question and answer and without which
the temporality of any plot is impossible), the detective story takes certain
features inherent in any narrative and concentrates its textual operations
upon their deployment; here, too, it exaggerates the reader's natural wish to
identify with the characters in a story and offers him one character in particular who fulfills the criteria of an ideal reader, but tends to deny him all

others. The reader of the detective novel, entranced by the impenetrable enigma of the figure of the detective, thereby forgets that he himself is a Narcissus, staring in wonder at the beauty of a disturbingly familiar face.

From this perspective, the difference between the English and the American traditions resides only in the way in which they conceptualize the activity of reading: for if the detective is a figure for the reader, different modes of detection can be construed as different implicit theories of reading. The English insulation of the detective from his case is designed to create one privileged discourse within the text that is capable of determining the value of all its other parts but that is not itself dependent upon them: the locus of truth is incarnated within the text in such a way that it can legislate to the other parts, so that it is in the text but not of it. Hence the tendency to unworldliness in the English detective, which contributes to his mystery and sometimes makes it difficult to imagine his existing in the same society as the other characters. His wisdom is essentially timeless, and his final correct understanding of the case takes the form of a momentary vision in which all its parts cohere: the time of the narrative of his investigation may mimic the temporality of reading but has none of the genuinely dialectic quality of the latter, none of its belatedness, duplicity, self-delusion, and hope. Unlike the American tradition, the English one can include the very short story, for the temporal deferral that separates crime from solution contributes in itself nothing to the latter and can be expanded, rearranged, or elided at will. It is this temporality of reading to which the American tradition accords so much importance: here the sequence of events may seem arbitrary but is, in fact, unalterable. Human time, in its despotic irreversibility, rules the American novels: the minor incident for which the detective is summoned must precede and cannot follow the murders that his entrance provokes, and his final account of the case takes the form of a narrative, of a chain of causes and effects in which the criminal became fettered more ineluctably the more desperately he sought to free himself. Here the detective is not the bearer of a higher wisdom but himself, at least in part, an imperfect agent. The threat of sex, like the actuality of violence, binds him to crimes for which he himself is in some sense responsible, for they would not have occurred (at least not in this way) if he had not entered the scene. His identification of the criminal is intended also to exculpate himself, but he can never be entirely freed of the burden of responsibility for having catalyzed the criminal's actions: at the end of each of these novels, Spade, Marlowe, or Archer is terribly alone, for these detectives embody that aspect of reading in which it is a guilty and solitary pleasure. Part of their mystery is that they continue in their professions at all, despite the bitterness of their knowledge of their world and of themselves.

Hence, the American tradition focuses upon the pain of the process of interpretation and the English upon the joy of its result. The English novelists presuppose the certainty of a correct reading and project back from that end to an initial stage of ignorance from which the path to that goal of knowledge is in principle never in doubt. The Americans, on the other hand, are caught up in the uncertainties of the activity of interpretation itself, for which a final and valid result may be imagined but can never be confidently predicted. From the point of view of the activity, the result is a utopia we may never attain; from the point of view of the result, the activity was meaningful only insofar as it led step by step to that end. The miracle of reading, and the dilemma of the mystery story, is that both are right.

II

In his book on the tragic drama of the German Baroque (a period that will be of importance for George Smiley), Walter Benjamin describes the difference between symbol and allegory in a way that casts light upon this contrast between the English and American traditions:

> Within the decisive category of time . . . the relation of symbol and allegory can be defined with an incisive formula. Whereas in the symbol destruction is idealized and the transfigured countenance of nature fleetingly reveals itself in the light of redemption, in allegory the observer is confronted with the *facies hippocratica* of history as a petrified, primordial landscape. History, in every regard in which, from the very beginning, it has been untimely, sorrowful, unsuccessful, expresses itself in a countenance—or rather in a death's head. . . . This is the heart of the allegorical way of seeing, of the baroque, secular explanation of history as the Passion of the world; it attains significance only in the stations of its decline.

Much of the conceptual framework Benjamin employs in this section of his book has striking affinities with the differences between the traditions of the detective novel outlined earlier: a literary theoretical distinction could easily be elaborated between the English authors' symbolic approach, with its non-historical and redemptively synthetic view, and the secular temporality of the Americans' allegory. Instead, I should like to call attention here to a new element this passage introduces, to the *facies hippocratica* Benjamin uses as a symbol for allegory. We may take Benjamin's hint and ask what kind of countenance the literary detective wears: more specifically, how he smiles.

The answer is only at first surprising. Within the English tradition, perhaps only Poe's Dupin almost never smiles: despite his chuckle in the passage quoted earlier, he is usually too much the romantic *poète maudit* to engage in levity, and the only people who laugh aloud in Poe's stories are fools who thereby betray their incomprehension. Elsewhere in this tradition, from Holmes through Poirot and Nero Wolfe, the detective smiles frequently:

> "It may seem very foolish in your eyes," I added, "but really I don't know how you deduced it."
> Holmes chuckled to himself.
> "I have the advantage of knowing your habits, my dear Watson," said he.

> "What is this, Holmes?" I cried. "This is beyond anything which I could have imagined."
> He laughed heartily at my perplexity.

> "Well, well, MacKinnon is a good fellow," said Holmes with a tolerant smile. "You can file it in our archives, Watson. Some day the true story may be told."

> Our visitor sprang from the chair. "What!" he cried, "you know my name?"
> "If you wish to preserve your incognito," said Holmes, smiling, "I would suggest that you cease to write your name upon the lining of your hat, or else that you turn the crown towards the person whom you are addressing."

This is the smile of wisdom, complacent in the superiority of its own power and tolerant of the weakness of mere humanity; the detective adopts it in the moment when he has understood something that no one else has, yet it signifies not only the incomparability of his skill but also the benevolence with which he will use it. Ultimately, this is the smile of the Greek gods in their epiphanies to mortals: the smile of Aphrodite asking Sappho what is bothering her now or the so-called "archaic smile" on countless early Greek statues. In terms of our earlier discussion, it is also the smile of the reader who can close the book with the mixture of delight and satisfaction that a full understanding of it brings.

This smile is never found on the faces of the detectives of Hammett, Chandler, or Macdonald: they lack the requisite benevolence no less than the necessary superiority. To be sure, they do smile upon occasion, but only in two ways. Rarely, they smile to deceive, to pretend to a man they do not trust that they trust him so that they can lure him into their clutches. But more commonly, their smile is wry, bitter, helpless in the face of the corruption of the world and of their own complicity in it; it is the sardonic smile of the reader who knows that his own life is no less ambiguous and stalemated than the novel he is now reading. In Raymond Chandler, the Hippocratic smile is a recurrent symbol: the rictus of death, it suggests a fullness of wisdom that only the dead can have and that therefore comes too late to be of any use to the living. Hippocrates should be able to heal; but the man who wears the Hippocratic smile is past healing. One time it is Marlowe himself who wears it. This happens at a crucial moment in *The Big Sleep*. Marlowe has just witnessed, helplessly from the next room, a gangster's callous murder of a fellow detective, Harry Jones. Marlowe is partly responsible for Jones's death: it was he, after all, who had told the gangster's boss that Jones was following him; and though Marlowe had certainly not intended this result, he will feel it necessary to expunge and compound his guilt for it, when the time comes, by gunning down the gangster without mercy in his turn. At the very end, in the eulogy to Rusty Regan, the only thoroughly decent man in the novel, whose corpse had already been decaying in a sump before the story had even begun, Marlowe will give voice to a deep envy for the dead, who have attained to a peace that the living seem foolish for so desperately deferring. But now the plot must go on: and it requires Marlowe to take over briefly the role of Jones, whose death was unnecessary and who in a sense died for him. Chandler writes:

> It was raining hard again. I walked into it with the heavy drops slapping my face. When one of them touched my tongue I knew that my mouth was open and the ache at the side of my jaws told me it was open wide and strained back, mimicking the rictus of death carved upon the face of Harry Jones.

III

Despite his name, George Smiley is not given much to smiling. Even at the moment of his greatest triumph, the forced defection of Karla at the end of *Smiley's People,* he does not share in the jubilation of his colleagues. Most often he seems worried, tentative; he blushes often; people think him confused and shy. These appearances both are and are not deceptive. For his name is no less carefully chosen than are those of Dupin, Sam Spade (direct and disillusioned, with the gravediggers' humor), Philip Marlowe (literate and endangered), and Lew Archer (a straight shooter and good guesser, a modern Apollo), and of most other literary detectives. As George, le Carré's hero is the slayer of the dragon, like his pseudonymous creator a defender of the faith, the guardian of traditional values. No wonder he is worried: for in a fallen world these can only be preserved by recourse to methods those same values must condemn. But as Smiley, he is not only put into contrast with such competing models of the secret agent as James Bond (can one imagine Ian Fleming's hero with Smiley's name?), but also placed firmly in the tradition of the literary detective, who, as we have learned to expect, ought by profession to smile. Why doesn't Smiley?

It may at first seem odd to consider Smiley a detective: after all, le Carré has attained celebrity as a writer of novels of espionage, and Smiley has entered the annals of world literature as a master spy. In fact, stories about spies and about detectives have much in common. As the two major subgenres of the thriller, they share many features: the interpretation of clues and the construction, revision, and eventual confirmation of hypotheses; an atmosphere of deceit, where treachery is the rule and trust a sometimes fatal mistake; a curious fascination with the many varieties of violent death. And historically, there have been many crossovers between the two modes: already Dupin's services were enlisted in affairs of state in "The Purloined Letter," as were Holmes's in "The Naval Treaty" and "His Last Bow"; and Nazi agents turn up in Chandler's *Lady in the Lake* and many other detective novels of the 1940s.

Yet considerable differences separate the modes of espionage and of mystery, and clarifying these will suggest the degree to which many of le Carré's novels, though full of spies, no less clearly belong to the tradition of detective fiction. These differences are not only thematic, in the sense in which we can say, for example, that mystery novels tend to center upon the destinies of individuals, whereas in spy novels the interests of nations are at stake. They are also, and even more clearly, formal. The plot of a mystery is retrospective: it looks backward to an event that happened before, at or shortly after its beginning, and, knowing that it has already occurred, asks how it happened. The plots of spy stories, on the other hand, tend to be prospective: they are directed toward an event that has not yet occurred and that must be either prevented (the threat against England must be warded off) or performed (the enemy must be given false information); they ask not who did it but what will happen. Because the event in a mystery has already occurred, the progress of its narrative is essentially a process of understanding, toward which the detective's actions are subordinated; because the event in a spy story has not yet happened, its hero must engage primarily in certain actions (to thwart or permit that event), and his gradually deepening understanding of the situation is valuable only insofar as it enables him to perform the decisive actions at the right moment. In a mystery, the culprit is identified only at the very end; in a spy story, the enemy can be known from the very beginning and the hero can be aware of his fiendish plan from a very early stage of the plot. Hence, the delay that is necessary for a narrative must be generated in a mystery story by the successive creation and refutation of interpretative models, whereas that in a spy story tends to take the form of temporary obstructions to the hero's freedom of action: whether he is captured, pursued, or injured by the enemy, the crucial point is that he be made incapable of fulfilling his mission at once. Usually, the motives for at least the original murder in a mystery are separate from the hero's activity of investigation: the murderer acted, at least the first time, from greed or jealousy, anger or revenge. In the spy novel, on the other hand, the victims are those who know too much, who could prevent the enemy's fulfilling his plan, and the hero is in no less danger than they were. If the spy story belongs to the genre of the picaresque novel (where the end is known in advance and is delayed by episodes) and goes back ultimately to the *Odyssey* (in which Odysseus acts over and over again the role of a spy), the mystery might be correlated with the folk form of the riddle (which begins with a question and ends with its answer) and has its classical forerunner in *Oedipus the King* (in which Oedipus is not only detective and judge but also criminal and, ultimately, victim).

An example will help to make the differences clearer. In John Buchan's *The Thirty-Nine Steps,* Scudder recounts to the hero, Hannay, in the very first chapter the full details of the plot to murder Karolides in London on July 15. This same chapter ends with the murder of Scudder, but Hannay's reaction is revealing:

> Somehow or other the sight of Scudder's dead face had made me a passionate believer in his scheme. He was gone, but he had taken me into his confidence, and I was pretty well bound to carry on his work. . . . I hate to see a good man downed, and that long knife would not be the end of Scudder if I could play the game in his place.

There is not a hint here of a desire to find the culprits and to bring them to justice: we have a murder, but not a mystery. To be sure, at the very end

Hannay will confront the foreign agents with a warrant for their arrest for the murder of Scudder; but we know that his intention is to prevent them from leaving the country with the details of the disposition of the British home fleet on mobilization and that this warrant is simply the most effective means available. Hannay knows from the beginning the enemy's intention to murder Karolides: the plot consists largely of a sequence of episodes entitled "Adventure," of pursuits, captivities, and escapes, in which the Black Stone try to track Hannay down and prevent him from thwarting their plans while the police seek him in connection with Scudder's murder (this latter element is the only aspect of the novel in which it approaches a mystery, but it is narrated from the point of view of the putative murderer, is largely tangential, and is never treated with full seriousness). In the end, it turns out that Karolides cannot be saved; but we have already learned that his death is inevitable and that the real danger comes from the planned betrayal of the naval secrets. This is the danger toward which the plot as a whole is directed; and it is one that Hannay succeeds in averting at the last minute.

With this in mind, we can return to le Carré and see that his novels fall easily into three categories: spy stories, mysteries that often involve spies, and a third and most interesting group, in which the two modes are played off against one another. That some of his works are more or less straightforward tales of espionage no one will deny. The plot of *The Looking Glass War* (1965), for example, is directed to the question of whether the East Germans are building a secret missile launching site. It turns out in the end that the indications that had seemed to point to this possibility had, in fact, been planted by Control in order to discredit a rival Ministry, and hence that the Head of the Circus is himself ultimately responsible for the murder of Taylor in the first chapter; but there is no murder investigation and no character who plays the role of the detective, and the question of who actually killed Taylor is barely raised and never answered. Again, *The Honourable Schoolboy* (1977) and *Smiley's People* (1979) are both directed toward bringing a foreign agent over into the West; though there are some extremely nasty murders, especially in the latter novel, those who die do so mostly because they knew too much, and the plots are aimed not toward the identification and punishment of the culprits but toward the final compromising and securing of the foreign agent; to this end the complex web of investigation, deception, and extortion is woven.

In the present context, more interest attaches to le Carré's mystery stories. It is often forgotten that le Carré began his literary career with two quite short novels, *Call for the Dead* (1961) and *A Murder of Quality* (1962): though both feature Smiley, only the former involves any other spies and

both are, in fact, best understood as detective novels. In *Call for the Dead,*
Smiley investigates the apparent suicide of a member of the Foreign Office
and discovers a series of anomalous circumstances that point unmistakably
to murder. For the rest of the novel, Smiley tracks the murderers until, in a
climactic confrontation, he himself kills the man who had ordered the diplomat slain. That this man was a foreign agent and that the diplomat had
been killed because he had come to suspect that his wife was a spy are of
little or no consequence for the plot of the novel (though they no doubt
contribute to its success in other regards). We have here, in essence, a
straightforward detective novel in the American tradition. Smiley has features
in this first novel that he will retain throughout his literary career and that
mark him as a familiar member of the ranks of literary detectives in general—
his enigmatic nature (the novel introduces Smiley by dwelling upon the inexplicability for English society of Lady Ann's marriage to him); his marginality in matters personal (symbolized by his predilection for German
literature, especially for the much-neglected Baroque period), marital (Lady
Ann's separation from him is announced on the first page), and professional
(in this, his first novel, he already retires from the Service); his cooperation
with the authorized institutions of investigation (embodied, not for the last
time, in Inspector Mendel) and his aloofness from them (indicated by his
refusal to accept the Service's offer to decline his letter of resignation). These
features would suffice to stamp Smiley as a detective; but others point no
less clearly to the heritage of Hammett and Chandler rather than to that of
Conan Doyle and Christie. Thus, Smiley becomes the victim of a physical
assault to which he almost succumbs; conversely, at the end he does not
arrest the criminal but instead slays him. Again, his participation in the case
involves him personally in other ways than those connected immediately with
the investigation: the head of the foreign agents had been Smiley's pupil
before the war, and, although this gives Smiley the knowledge that enables
him to lay a successful trap, it also means that, when Smiley kills him, he
will be overwhelmed by remorse and self-loathing:

> Dieter was dead, and he had killed him. The broken fingers of
> his right hand, the stiffness of his body and the sickening head-
> ache, the nausea of guilt, all testified to this. And Dieter had let
> him do it, had not fired the gun, had remembered their friendship
> when Smiley had not. . . . They had come from different hemi-
> spheres of the night, from different worlds of thought and con-
> duct. Dieter, mercurial, absolute, had fought to build a
> civilization. Smiley, rationalistic, protective, had fought to prevent

him. "Oh God," said Smiley aloud, "who was then the gentleman."

Such passages are characteristic of the American tradition, where in the end
there may be little difference between detective and criminal beyond the fact
that the former succeeds at the cost of the latter: is there any doubt at the
end of a mystery by Christie or Sayers who the gentleman was? But the most
telling evidence for assigning *Call for the Dead* to the American tradition of
detective fiction derives from the structure of its plot. For Smiley is brought
in, not after the murder, but before it, and the murder is a direct result of
his introduction into the story. An anonymous letter had been received,
denouncing the diplomat as a former communist, and Smiley had been ordered to interview him. One of the ironies of the plot is that the matter was
thoroughly trivial, and Smiley saw no reason to pursue the investigation; but
a foreign agent had observed the two walking in a park together, had concluded that the diplomat would betray them, and had decided he must be
killed. Another irony becomes obvious at the end, when it turns out that the
agent was right: the anonymous letter had been written by the diplomat
himself, not in order to jeopardize his career but so as to establish a first
contact with Smiley's Service.

To turn from *Call for the Dead* to *A Murder of Quality* is to move from
the American to the English tradition of mystery stories. This is le Carré's
purest detective novel: its plot could have come directly out of Agatha Christie. The case involves the murder of the wife of a faculty member at an
exclusive boys' school; Smiley enters it only because she had written, ex-
pressing fears for her life, to a friend of his. The murder occurs before he
arrives; he solves it with the help of the local police; at the end, the murderer
is arrested. To be sure, le Carré uses the novel as a vehicle to explore the
social and psychological tensions arising from contemporary changes in English life, and a kind of negative personal complicity on the part of Smiley
in the case he is investigating is established by the repeated references to
Lady Ann, who belongs to the social class of which the school is part in a
way that Smiley never will; but, in terms of its plot, the novel is thoroughly
conventional. It almost gives the impression that le Carré, at the beginning
of his career, had deliberately chosen to apprentice himself first in the one
tradition and then in the other before going on to more serious work.

The results are evident in le Carré's most interesting mystery novel,
Tinker, Tailor, Soldier, Spy (1974). Here the plot has the form of a murder
mystery, although the victim, Jim Prideaux, did not die but was (only) shot,
captured, and tortured. There are four suspects, four highly placed officials

in the Circus who could have been the Russian agent responsible for the betrayal of Prideaux's mission; and Smiley is brought out of retirement in order to determine which of the four is the guilty party by investigative procedures no different from those any traditional detective would use. Moreover, the clue that firmly establishes the guilt of Bill Haydon is of the most conventional sort:

> "Sam, listen. Bill was making love to Ann that night. No, listen. You phoned her, she told you Bill wasn't there. As soon as she'd rung off, she pushed Bill out of bed and he turned up at the Circus an hour later knowing that there had been a shooting in Czecho. If you were giving me the story from the shoulder—on a postcard—that's what you'd say?"
>
> "Broadly."
>
> "But you didn't tell Ann about Czecho when you phoned her—"
>
> "He stopped at his club on the way to the Circus."
>
> "If it was open. Very well: then why didn't he know that Jim Prideaux had been shot?"

This is only the slightest of variations upon the traditional scene in which the criminal, told the victim has been murdered, blurts out, "My God, who shot him?" and the detective murmurs, "Who said anything of his being shot?"

But this passage occurs only two-thirds of the way through the novel. Why, then, is Haydon not arrested at once? The reason casts light upon the way le Carré has modified the conventions of the mystery novel to suit his purposes. It will be recalled that the American tradition permits the detective's personal complicity in the case to become an important factor in the plot: here le Carré develops this feature ingeniously by having Bill Haydon become notoriously adulterous with Lady Ann. It was no accident that Haydon had been in bed with Smiley's wife on the night Prideaux was shot. For if Smiley were to finger Haydon on the basis of the kind of evidence just cited, it would be thought he was acting out of jealousy: this had been part of Karla's design. Hence, Smiley must create a trap in which some new action of Haydon's will prove his guilt beyond any possible doubt; and the last part of the novel is devoted to his setting this trap.

Another problem remains, however. If *Tinker, Tailor, Soldier, Spy* is, in fact, formally a murder mystery, why was Jim Prideaux not murdered? Why is the victim permitted to survive? Le Carré's innovation in this regard moves the detective novel beyond the realm of ordinary crime and inserts it into a specifically political context. For what is to be done with Haydon once he has been identified as the foreign agent? In the traditional criminal novel, the murderer's death or arrest provides an entirely satisfactory conclusion; but here both alternatives are quite problematic. For the English Service to kill Haydon would taint Smiley in a way le Carré is elsewhere at pains to avoid. On the other hand, political considerations would require Haydon to be imprisoned and eventually sent to the East in exchange for some captured Western spy; yet, given the enormity of Haydon's betrayal, such an ending would violate the reader's sense of justice and seem intolerably weak. The demands of justice can only be satisfied if Haydon can be appropriately punished; and Prideaux's murder of Haydon, in spite of all of Smiley's precautionary measures, cleverly provides a satisfactory conclusion to the novel without implicating Smiley.

The last three novels we have considered can all be adequately interpreted in terms of their use of traditional mystery plots; but already in the third one we have seen how certain features point beyond the limits of that genre. In conclusion, I should like to turn to two other novels by le Carré in which the central categories of the mystery tradition are employed only so that they can be radically put into question.

The Spy Who Came In from the Cold (1963) begins with the death of an agent in Berlin. When Alec Leamas, his contact, returns to England, Control proposes to him a plan whereby the man responsible for the murder can be punished. Leamas accepts the plan because of his desire to avenge the agent's death upon the man who ordered it, the East German agent Mundt:

> "That is, of course, if you're *sure you want* to . . . no mental fatigue or anything?"
> "If it's a question of killing Mundt, I'm game."

> "He said there was a job he'd got to do. Someone to pay off for something they'd done to a friend of his."

Leamas, like the reader, is convinced that he is involved in a typical mystery plot: the guilty will be brought to justice and the moral order will be restored. There is, to be sure, no detection (Mundt's guilt is clear from the beginning), and the plot is prospective insofar as it is directed toward the eventual compromising of the East German: yet reader and hero always look backward as they move forward and envision that ending as a satisfactory answer to the problem posed by the beginning. But, of course, it is revealed in the end that Leamas, and we with him, have been deceived: the object of Control's plot turns out to have been the death not of Mundt (who was, in fact, an English agent) but of his subordinate Fiedler (who had been on the point of discovering Mundt's treason and himself acts the role of the detective within Control's elaborate scheme). The conventions of the mystery story are used as a red herring to deceive the reader as well as the characters and they are exploded by the ending, in which the murderer is saved while the East German detective and the English avenger are killed. Le Carré takes considerable pains to establish Mundt's vile and vicious character—in contrast to him, not only Leamas but also Fiedler are thoroughly sympathetic figures—and the resulting jolt to the reader's sensibilities helps to make the novel's ending so fully and satisfactorily unsettling. But the contribution le Carré's inversion of the generic conventions of the mystery novel makes to achieving this effect ought not to be neglected: to discover that the search for truth and justice is not the real object but only a ruse to protect their opposites for reasons of national self-interest provides an ingenious surprise by purely formal means. To be sure, the traditional American mystery had allowed the possibility that society was so corrupt that the detective's uncovering of the truth could no longer save it: Marlowe's Southern California is in many ways irredeemable, and, at the end of *The Big Sleep*, the small fry can be punished but Eddy Mars retains his nefarious power, and the murder of Rusty Regan may be brought to light but is immediately hushed up. Yet, by turning those who believe in the ideals of detection into naive pawns in the hands of the cynical practitioners of realpolitik, *The Spy Who Came In from the Cold* pushes Chandler's moral disillusionment an important step farther. Le Carré's novel implicitly asks the question whether English society has not reached the point at which the truth must be suppressed and justice thwarted if the society is to be preserved. In terms of literary genres, this can be translated into the question whether the mystery story is still possible in our time.

It is to this question that le Carré's *A Small Town in Germany* (1968) is most systematically addressed. The plot begins when Leo Harting, an employee at the British Embassy in Bonn, vanishes; he has taken sensitive files with him, and the suspicion of his defection is immediately invoked. Alan Turner is sent from England to track him down, and we seem to be confronted with a standard mystery in which the detective (Turner) pursues the criminal (Harting). But in the course of Turner's investigation a surprising truth emerges: Harting is evidently not a spy for the East but has himself been investigating the background of an important West German political figure, Karfeld. Eventually, it becomes clear that Karfeld had committed an atrocity during the Second World War and that Harting had come upon the traces of his crime. Instead of the detective (Turner) pursuing the criminal (Harting), we find one detective (Turner) pursuing another detective (Harting) who, in turn, is pursuing the real criminal (Karfeld). The differences between the two detectives are obvious. Harting, "the memory man," is obsessed with discovering the truth about the past and with seeing justice done; no consideration of policy or of self-interest can prevent him from bending every effort to investigating the traces of a crime and to seeing to it that the man who bears the guilt for it is appropriately punished. In his moral rigor, unswerving determination, and investigative ingenuity, Harting is the perfect type of the classic literary detective. Turner, on the other hand, is bound by considerations of national policy: for the English have formed a secret alliance with Karfeld, based on mutual self-interest, and are desperately concerned that the German politician not be discredited. Turner is himself too much a detective not to feel a powerful sympathy with Harting and to try his best not to obstruct him; but in the end he cannot prevent Harting from being killed and Karfeld from being saved. The war criminal can continue in his meteoric political career; the interests of England are protected; but the authentic detective is murdered and the inauthentic one is condemned to futility and self-hatred. Turner's last conversation with the diplomat Bradfield, who incarnates the cynicism of power in the novel, establishes its ultimate frame of reference:

> Turner searched frantically around him. "It's not true! You *can't* be so tied to the surface of things."
>
> "What else is there when the underneath is rotten? Break the surface and we sink. That's what Harting has done. I am a hypocrite," he continued simply. "I'm a great believer in hypocrisy. It's the nearest we ever get to virtue. It's a statement of what we ought to be. Like religion, like art, like the law, like marriage. I serve the appearance of things. . . . He *has* offended," he added casually, as if passing the topic once more in review. "Yes. He has. Not as much against myself as you might suppose. But against the order that results from chaos; against the built-in moderation of an aimless society. He had no business to hate Karfeld and none to. . . . He had no business to remember. If you and I have a purpose at all anymore, it is to save the world from such presumptions."
>
> "Of all of you—listen!—of all of you he's the only one who's real, the only one who believed, and acted! For you it's a sterile,

rotten game, a family word game, that's all—just play. But Leo's *involved*! He knows what he wants and he's gone to get it!"

"Yes. That alone should be enough to condemn him."

If modern society is directed solely to the future rather than to the past, if the necessary and sufficient goal of national policy is survival, if the appearances must be preserved because there is nothing else besides them, what place can remain for the detective who seeks to decipher the enigma of the past, whatever the cost for the present? At the end of Chandler's novels, Marlowe may be condemned to futility; at the end of le Carré's novel, Harting is condemned to death. Marlowe may don the Hippocratic smile; Harting can no longer doff it. In the murder of Harting is figured the death of the traditional mystery novel. Authors may continue to write detective novels; le Carré himself has done so. But the insight to which le Carré has given voice in *A Small Town in Germany* may well anticipate the end of the genre. Future generations may no longer understand why the past century has been so obsessed with the discovery of truth and the punishment of crime. For them, the mystery novel may become mysterious in a way we would prefer not to envision.

LARS OLE SAUERBERG

Fear of Extremes: England's Relationship with Germany and America

In le Carré's two earliest secret-agent stories, *Call for the Dead* and *The Spy Who Came In from the Cold,* the only countries involved are England and Eastern Germany. It is not until *A Small Town in Germany* (1968) that the English relationship to friendly nations receives attention. In that story le Carré thematizes Anglo-German relations, past and present, to suggest something about the nature of incipient fascism.

At the beginning of the story le Carré has a Whitehall civil servant express the conventional view of the Germans; a view probably shared with many readers: "A nation of psychopaths. Always think that they are being got at. Versailles, encirclement, stab in the back; persecution mania, that's their trouble." As the action progresses it becomes increasingly clear that such a view is too simple to explain the present situation. The keyword for a thematic interpretation of the story is *illusion,* and nationalistic prejudice is as much an illusion as Harting's conviction that the truth about Karfeld must be brought out, at any cost. The diplomatic endeavour to pave the way for English membership is based on a realization that illusions must be played against each other if the goal is to be reached. The British negotiation potential is in the illusion of military strength: Bradfield explains the situation to the hero:

> "Hear me out. There is something here that does not exist in England. It is called the anti-Soviet alliance. The Germans take it

---

From *Secret Agents in Fiction: Ian Fleming, John le Carré and Len Deighton.* © 1984 by Lars Ole Sauerberg. Macmillan, 1984.

very seriously, and we deride it at our peril: *it is still our ticket to Brussels*. For twenty years or more, we have dressed ourselves in the shining armour of the defender. We may be bankrupt, we may beg for loans, currency and trade; we may occasionally . . . reinterpret . . . our Nato commitments; when the guns sound, we may even bury our heads under the blankets; our leaders may be as futile as theirs."

What was it Turner discerned in Bradfield's voice at that moment? Self-disgust? a ruthless sense of his own decline? He spoke like a man who had tried all remedies, and would have no more of doctors. For a moment the gap between them had closed, and Turner heard his own voice speaking through the Bonn mist.

"For all that, in terms of popular psychology, it is the one great unspoken strength we have: that when the Barbarians come from the East, the Germans may count on our support. That Rhine Army will hastily gather on the Kentish hills and the British independent nuclear deterrent will be hustled into service."

The events of the story suggest, however, that the status of England has already deteriorated to an extent which makes the confidence in the nuclear deterrent obsolete. Karfeld's appeal to the Germans is extremely successful, and at the same time Siebkron, the leader of the police, sees his chance to consolidate his own role in the confusion which is the result of the passivity of a weak government and the appeal of extra-parliamentary voices. Against this background it is unlikely that the English are seen by the Germans as the ultimate protector, and Karfeld receives loud applause when he blames Britain for oppression, cultural and military.

As I suggested [elsewhere], le Carré's justification of his heroes' activities is in their humanistic endeavour: avoidance of extremes and allowance for human frailty. As Dieter Frey in *Call for the Dead* was blamed for his pursuit of the absolute, the Germany imagined in *A Small Town in Germany* represents a similar pursuit, but on a national scale. In the middle of the budding fascism is Bonn, which is emphasized again and again as a "world in exile." Bonn may be interpreted to symbolize mere potentiality: it may be subject to influence, but is as yet undecided. It is a town of mists.

In the diplomatic quarter of Bonn the English embassy personnel have their enclave. It is a perfect model of a middle-class London suburb, and it symbolizes the potential perversion of le Carré's humanistic ideals, a self-satisfactory and complacent middle-of-the-road attitude to existence. The fictional Germany has chosen the road to fascism, because this is one way to assert its existence as a nation, but it is a way which is obviously the result of a feeling of victimization combined with delusions of grandeur. Both premises are latent in the bitter and desperate attitudes expressed by members of the English colony in Bonn, notably Bradfield and de Lisle. Bonn is the test of Karfeld's movement as well as of the English attitude to a situation which is, in many ways, similar to the German.

The role played by the USA receives increasing attention in the course of le Carré's work. When in *The Spy Who Came In from the Cold* Leamas angrily states to his first defection contact that he has been an "Office boy for the bloody Yanks," he is, of course, supposed to vent his anger as a motive to defection. But at the same time the bitter utterance serves as a prelude to what becomes a major theme in the Karla trilogy. Also in *The Looking Glass War* there is a brief reference to the superiority of the Americans, but as this story is ironic throughout as regards anachronistic concepts of national importance, Leclerc's exegesis must be read as le Carré's wish to ask the reader to face reality:

> "The Minister was anxious that we shouldn't alarm them prematurely. One only has to suggest rockets to the Americans to get the most drastic action. Before we know where they are they'll be flying U-2s over Rostock." Encouraged by their laughter, Leclerc continued "The Minister made another point which I think I might pass on to you. The Minister made another point which I think I might pass on to you. The country which comes under maximum threat from these rockets—they have a range of around eight hundred miles—might well be our own. It is certainly not the United States. Politically, this would be a bad moment to go hiding our faces in the Americans' skirts. After all, as the Minister put it, we still *have* one or two teeth of our own."

As in the three previous stories, the USA is not directly involved in *A Small Town in Germany,* but whereas America was mentioned in *The Spy Who Came In from the Cold* and *The Looking Glass War* as the potential contributor to the action, it is referred to here for the values it represents. De Lisle reflects on the interior of the American Club in Bonn:

> "Is *all* America like this?" de Lisle enquired. "Or worse?" He looked slowly round. "Though it does give a sense of *dimension,* I suppose. And optimism. That's the trouble with Americans, isn't it really? All that emphasis on the future. So dangerous. It makes them destructive of the present. Much kinder to look *back,* I always think. I see no hope for the future, and it gives me a

great sense of freedom. And of caring: We're much nicer to one
another in the condemned cell aren't we? Don't take me too
seriously, will you?"

De Lisle's observations on America in the passage quoted above may be read
both as the restating of le Carré's belief in the redeeming power of the past
and as the prelude to the role America is to play in the trilogy. If fascism is
one danger threatening England, "Americanism" is another.

The critical attitude towards America reaches its culmination in *The
Honourable Schoolboy,* but the road is paved carefully in *Tinker, Tailor,
Soldier, Spy.* Like le Carré's other stories this one is based on actual fact.
Le Carré has allowed his imagination to work on the likely developments of
the treason scandals in Britain since the war, in particular the Philby affair.
The plot of *Tinker, Tailor, Soldier, Spy* is formed by Smiley's endeavours to
reveal the identity of a Russian mole at the highest level in the Circus, and
this makes it possible for le Carré to consider political values from various
angles. As I suggested [elsewhere], the Smiley of this story is not very certain
about absolute political convictions; his anger is aroused by Haydon's breach
of loyalty and calculated lies rather than patriotic and political considerations. The lines are drawn up sharply in the former agent Jim Prideaux's
appreciation of the general political situation. Jim Prideaux, it must be remembered, is a fieldman in many ways similar to Leamas of *The Spy Who
Came In from the Cold,* and, in addition to his lack of nuanced political
views, he is bitter about his own personal fate:

> To the West, America, he said, full of greedy fools fouling up
> their inheritance. To the East, China-Russia, he drew no distinc-
> tion: boiler suits, prison camps, and a damn long march to no-
> where. In the middle . . .

But Jim Prideaux's attitude to the Americans is, despite his lack of sophistication, like de Lisle's in *A Small Town in Germany*: both emphasize the
Americans' carelessness about the past. The values represented by Prideaux's
oblique reference to Britain by his "In the middle . . ." are given substance
by Smiley's ironic consideration of himself as a "soft fool" and the "very
archetype of a flabby Western liberal." Smiley's liberalism is the bulwark
against the USA as well as against the Soviet Union. Smiley, however, has no
illusions that his assignment to reveal the mole is ultimately a service to the
Americans:

> "An American connection, a big American dividend I mean,
> would put the mole Gerald *right* at the top table. The Circus, too,

by proxy of course. As a Russian, one would give almost anything to the English if . . . well, if one could buy the Americans in return."

There is a streak of jealousy in Smiley's summary of the situation which anticipates the obvious state of competition in *The Honourable Schoolboy*, and it sets the key for the attitude to the Americans that the last observations on the trans-Atlantic ally are put into the mouth of Haydon, the traitor. His words are mechanical repetitions of ideological articles of faith, and thus repellent to Smiley's individualism, but Smiley does not question their basic message:

> The statement began with a long apologia, of which he [Smiley] afterwards recalled only a few sentences:
> "We live in an age where only fundamental issues matter . . ."
> "The United States is no longer capable of undertaking its own revolution . . ."
> "The political posture of the United Kingdom is without relevance or moral viability in world affairs . . ."
> With much of it, Smiley might in other circumstances have agreed: it was the tone, rather than the music, which alienated him.
> "In capitalist America economic repression of the masses is institutionalised to a point which not even Lenin could have foreseen . . ."
> "The cold war began in 1917, but the bitterest struggles lie ahead of us, as America's deathbed paranoia drives her to greater excesses abroad."

The result of Haydon's betrayal is that the English Secret Service has to begin its activities from scratch, which means that the situation in *The Honourable Schoolboy* is one of "fatal dependence upon their American sister service."

The general symbol of America in *The Honourable Schoolboy* is money. Smiley makes no secret of his economic dependence on the CIA, but at the same time he implies that the English force is quality which cannot be replaced by quantity; but quality cannot emerge without economic support. Smiley states the problem neatly: "If we don't, we've no resources. It's simply a matter of balance." There is a faint but distinct echo in this implied distribution of spiritual and material values from Bond's defence of British virtues in *You Only Live Twice*. The difference between British and American approaches agrees well with le Carré's favourite theme of pretense versus

sincerity and its corollary of the past versus the present. The settings in
which the combined meetings between the Circus and the CIA take place
illustrate the difference between the economic capabilities of the two services:

> Before the fall, studiously informal meetings of intelligence part-
> ners to the special relationship were held as often as monthly and
> followed by what Smiley's predecessor Alleline had liked to call
> "a jar." If it was the American turn to play host, then Alleline
> and his cohorts, among them the popular Bill Haydon, would be
> shepherded to the vast rooftop bar, known within the Circus as
> the planetarium, to be regaled with dry martinis and a view of
> West London they could not otherwise have afforded. If it was
> the British turn, then a trestle table was set up in the rumpus
> room, and a darned damask tablecloth spread over it, and the
> American delegates were invited to pay homage to the last bastion
> of clubland spying, and incidentally the birthplace of their own
> service, while they sipped South African sherry disguised by cut-
> glass decanters on the grounds that they wouldn't know the dif-
> ference.

In the description of the chief's office in the CIA's London headquarters
le Carré manages to evoke associations which are definitely negative in Smiley's perspective: emphasis on money, ostentatious nationalism and imper-
sonality. It is also interesting that the way Martello, the CIA chief, dresses
is incongruous, and that the presence of two assistants may lead the reader
to compare this scene with, for instance, the scene in Fleming's *Live and Let
Die* where Bond is taken to see the gangster chief, Mr Big. The Italian name
of the CIA chief may be intended to give associations to the Mafia:

> The doors, incidentally, were double, with black grilles over black
> iron, and gilded feathers on the grilles. The cost of them alone
> would have kept the entire Circus ticking over for a couple more
> days at least. Once inside them, [Smiley and Guillam] had the
> sensation of coming from a hamlet to a metropolis.
>
> Martello's room was very large. There were no windows and
> it could have been midnight. Above an empty desk an American
> flag, unfurled as if by a breeze, occupied half the end wall. At
> the centre of the floor a ring of airline chairs was clustered round
> a rosewood table, and in one of these sat Martello himself, a
> burly, cheerful-looking Yale man in a country suit which seemed

always out of season. Two quiet men flanked him, each as sallow
and sincere as the other.

One of the things noted by Smiley in Martello's office is a portrait of Richard
Nixon, although, as Smiley reflects, "Nixon had resigned a good six months
ago." The presence of the former president's portrait may, of course, be due
to negligence, but that is hardly the case in the otherwise efficient American
embassy. A more likely possibility is that le Carré wishes to indicate a certain
unwillingness on the part of the CIA to say goodbye to a president who, as
it turned out, preferred clandestine channels to a more open kind of government.

In many ways the USA assumes the role of adversary in *The Honourable
Schoolboy* because Smiley has to compete with the ally throughout, and
eventually he is outwitted in a conspiracy initiated by some of his own
colleagues in association with the CIA. In the fictional universe of this story
the Americans represent values which are in fundamental disagreement with
Smiley's.

In accordance with the thematic changes in *Smiley's People,* the importance of international relations is reduced to almost nil. Although there are
many geographical shifts in the story (France, Denmark, Germany, Switzerland) the countries visited by Smiley remain of plot-structural values only
(chapters 3 and 6). Smiley's assignment is in this story a purely personal
crusade to get even with Karla, the man who engineered the destruction of
the Circus. The impression that the reader gets of nations friendly to England
is nothing more than the descriptive detail necessary to create a minimum
of atmosphere. The superiority of the English Secret Service over the CIA is
implied in the circumstance that the success is Smiley's, but the state of
competition so obvious in *The Honourable Schoolboy* is absent as a theme
in *Smiley's People.*

Despite the substitution of England by Israel in *The Little Drummer
Girl* and the consequent disappearance of the USA as the jealous friend ready
to step in with superior force but inferior brains, Germany once again plays
a major part. The opening pages of the book describe the diplomats' suburbia
in Bonn which we recognize from *A Small Town in Germany,* and another
note of recognition is struck with the introduction of a high-ranking security
policeman constantly referred to by the area of his origin, the Silesian. This
heavy, unimaginative and tactless officer is a personification of the renewed
drive towards fascism as described in *A Small Town in Germany.* Le Carré's
strong dislike of this particular aspect of what in more romantic times than
ours could have been called its *Volksseele* is voiced partly through this car-

icature, partly through his superior Dr. Alexis. Although Dr. Alexis is a more faceted figure than the Silesian it only means that le Carré's criticism of the new Bundesrepublik can be carried out with a subtlety more suitable to the author's quiet irony than the musical-comedy directness with which the Silesian performs.

Naturally, there is a certain delicacy in the relations between the Israeli agents and their German counterparts. In le Carré's fictional universe the Germans are taken for several rides by Kurtz and his men. In comparison with Kurtz, who is constantly exposed to danger and forced to make decisions about life and death, Dr. Alexis enjoys an existence comfortably removed from any disturbance apart from investigations of the occasional terrorist bomb. There is something uncannily ludicrous about the way that emphasis is put on the "clean" lineage of Dr. Alexis as regards the Holocaust, as if Germans, or indeed other human beings, may be divided into two mutually exclusive groups of tainted and untainted. Just as the Nazi rulers dictated the study of lines of descent to detect Jewish ancestry, the modern Germany carries on the identical procedure, admittedly for different purposes, but with the same faith in absolutism and thoroughness. In addition to this major indictment of the new Germany in the person of Dr. Alexis, the reader will note the doctor's fondness for external appearance, his glib and superficial nature so useful for the demands of mass society, and hypocrisy in his dealings with the Israelis. Dr. Alexis is quite willing to harvest from the Israeli progress, but claims ethical scruples when his involvement is required, a claim, however, which obviously enjoys lower priority than his financial interests.

Dr. Alexis is, of course, a fictional character and should be considered as such, but seen against le Carré's earlier portraits of Western Germany there can be little doubt that he is being used to represent national characteristics as well.

In le Carré's stories Germany and the USA tend to assume symbolic importance, and it is impossible to consider their value as symbols without at the same time considering le Carré's sense of ethical values as they are expressed mainly in the figure of Smiley. The Germany of *A Small Town in Germany* and the USA of *Tinker, Tailor, Soldier, Spy* and *The Honourable Schoolboy* represent developments which are potential developments of Western countries, including England. Both are, in le Carré's perspective, perversions of a truly humanistic development because both countries symbolize the excess which is anathema to the "flabby Western liberal" in the figure of Smiley. If *Smiley's People* is meant as the exit of Smiley for good, the thematic pattern of the trilogy is a move away from severe criticism of the development preferred by the USA to what may be considered complete dis-illusionment as regards the checking of potentially pernicious political de-velopments. There is a striking similarity between the frustration of Turner at the end of *A Small Town in Germany* when he witnesses the force of Karfeld's hordes and the frustration of Smiley at the end of *The Honourable Schoolboy*: both men are powerless before the values represented by Karfeld's movement and the USA respectively. Turner tries to act, but is stopped in the attempt (by the German police!), and Smiley resigns. When le Carré's hero returns in *Smiley's People,* international politics have been abandoned as the motivation for his action and are only left as a facade that justifies what is essentially his private effort to prove the superiority of himself to Karla.

WILLIAM F. BUCKLEY, JR.

Terror and a Woman:
The Little Drummer Girl

The beginning of John le Carré's new book is, for a spy thriller, entirely orthodox: There is a bombing, a bombing by a terrorist. Where? Near Bonn, but the location does not matter. There have been so many others, in Zurich, in Leyden, here and there. It matters only that the victim was an Israeli. Although the reader spends time in Bonn and in Tel Aviv and in Vienna, Munich, Mykonos, London, it matters hardly at all, except that the ambiance of these places is an invitation for Mr. le Carré to use his palette. The places are simply where the terrorist strikes, or where the antiterrorists are collected.

It becomes instantly apparent that we are in the hands of a writer of great powers. In the very first paragraph of *The Little Drummer Girl* he reveals the skill with which he can write in shorthand: "It was the Bad Godesberg incident that gave the proof. . . . Before Bad Godesberg, there had been growing suspicion; a lot of it. But the high quality of the planning, as against the poor quality of the bomb, turned the suspicion into certainty. Sooner or later, they say in the trade, a man will sign his name."

And then Mr. le Carré informs the reader that he is in no hurry at all; he has all the time in the world. So he gives us a little belletrism, and that also works. He describes the residential diplomatic area in which the bombing took place: "The fronts of some of the houses were already half obscured by dense plantations of conifers, which, if they ever grow to proper size, will presumably one day plunge the whole area into a Grimm's fairy-tale black-

From *The New York Times Book Review,* 13 March 1983. © 1983 by The New York Times Co.

out." There is the "patently nationalistic" look of some of the dwellings. "The Norwegian Ambassador's residence, for example, just around the corner from the Drosselstrasse, is an austere, redbricked farmhouse lifted straight from the stockbroker hinterlands of Oslo. The Egyptian consulate, up the other end, has the forlorn air of an Alexandrian villa fallen on hard times. Mournful Arab music issues from it, and its windows are permanently shuttered against the skirmishing North African heat."

We are very quickly aware that we are reading not Dashiell Hammett but someone much more like Lawrence Durrell. The author does not forget his duty. There is sleuthing galore ahead of the reader; and, in the end, the Palestinian terrorist is emphatically dead. But the momentum of the story is not ended with his death. There is left—the girl. The instrument of the Israeli antiterrorists. An English actress named Charlie, she is permanently changed by the complex role imposed on her—to be faithful at once to the Israeli and the Palestinian causes. And she is in love with the most mysterious character to have appeared in recent fiction, whose flesh-and-blood reification Mr. le Carré flatly refuses to give us. His name is Joseph, and other than the Israeli superspy Schulmann, the English actress Charlie and, however briefly, the Palestinian superterrorist Khalil, there is only Joseph seriously to ponder. At first he is merely a will-o'-the-wisp, and one is not entirely certain that he actually exists. Then he is incorporated formally into the plot, his persona on the one hand central, on the other hand continuingly elusive. And when finally only he exists for Charlie, after the entrapment, after Khalil is gone, the magnetism is enormous. The emotional tension of the postlude elevates it into a full fourth act. A wonderful achievement.

Mr. le Carré's novel is certainly the most mature, inventive and powerful book about terrorists-come-to-life this reader has experienced. It transcends the genre by reason of the will and the interests of the author. The story line interests him but does not dominate him. He is interested in writing interestingly about things interesting and not interesting. Terrorism and counterterrorism, intelligence work and espionage are, then, merely the vehicle for a book about love, anomie, cruelty, determination, and love of country. *The Little Drummer Girl* is about spies as *Madame Bovary* is about adultery or *Crime and Punishment* about crime. Mr. le Carré easily establishes that he is not beholden to the form he elects to use. This book will permanently raise him out of the espionage league, narrowly viewed.

I venture this judgment even though I am not familiar with all of his preceding books. Indeed I remember discarding one of them as too steep, in my cursory scouting of its first couple of chapters, to be worth climbing, pending the judgment of others I had confidence in that the view would be worth the effort. *Drummer Girl* has here and there passages that demand diligent reading. And sometimes Mr. le Carré is drawn, annoyingly, to non-declarative narrative. Disdain for narrative rigidity is probably closer. There is something of John Fowles in his style, in the liberties he gives himself to wander about as he likes, to dwell at any length that grips him or amuses him, serenely confident as he is that we will be, respectively, gripped and amused—and if not, we should go read other people's books. But he succeeds, almost always, because he is naturally expressive, dominant and in turn dominating in his use of language. And so the liberties he takes tend to be accepted as a part of his tapestry—even if, looked at discretely, they can be, as I say, annoying and even logically dissonant.

Here is an example. The Israeli Schulmann, determined to track down the Palestinian Khalil, has decided (most implausibly) on the attractive instrument for the entrapment—the touring actress, half-gypsy, half flower child, Charlie. And so he kidnaps her and begins a brainwashing operation that in most circumstances would cause the reader to smile with condescending incredulity. Consider the girl being interrogated thoroughly so that the supersleuth can learn literally all he can about her, the better to manipulate the penetration of the terrorist network.

It is known that Charlie's childhood home was taken by creditors when her father was caught up in embezzlement, and the supersleuth presses her for details of the episode:

> "Charlie, we recognize that this is very painful for you, but we ask you to continue in your own words. We have the van. We see your possessions leaving the house. What else do we see?"
> "My pony."
> "They took that too?"
> "I told you already."
> "With the furniture? In the same van?"
> "No, a separate one. Don't be bloody silly."
> "So there were two vans. Both at the same time? Or one after the other?"
> "I don't remember."

Charlie was quite right. The questioner was being bloody silly. But wait.

About the same man who could ask bloody silly questions, Mr. le Carré can write, "When Schulmann smiled, the wrinkles that flew into his face had been made by centuries of water flowing down the same rock paths and his eyes clamped narrow like a Chinaman's. Then, long after him, his sidekick smiled, echoing some twisted inner meaning. . . . When Schulmann talked, he fired off conflicting ideas like a spread of bullets, then waited to see which ones went home and which came back at him. The sidekick's voice followed like a stretcher party, softly collecting the dead." People who merit such description can be forgiven occasional silliness.

Is there a message in *Drummer Girl*? Yes. A quite earnest one. It is that the intensity with which the Israelis defend what they have got can only be understood if one understands the intensity with which the Palestinians resent what it is that they have lost. The Israelis triumph in the novel, even as they do in life. But Mr. le Carré is careful to even up the moral odds. I have in the past been discomfited by trendy ventures in ideological egalitarianism, such that the reader ends by finding the Communist spy and the Western spy equally weak, equally heroic; and perhaps the ambiguist in Mr. le Carré would overcome him in any exercise in which the alternative was moral polarization. But having acknowledged that this may be in John le Carré a temperamental weakness, reflecting the clutch of ambiguity rather than any ultimate fear of moral fine-tuning, one must go on to acknowledge that he permits the Palestinian point to be made with rare and convincing eloquence.

He is a very powerful writer. His entertainment is of a high order. He gives pleasure in his use of language. And his moral focus is interesting and provocative.

DAVID MONAGHAN

"A World Grown Old
and Cold and Weary":
Description as Metaphor

Action and character dominate John le Carré's novels. Passages of description are therefore relatively infrequent and usually brief. Nevertheless, their
importance should not be underrated. Le Carré may be sparing in his evo-
cations of building, place and landscape, but he is also remarkably consistent
and purposeful, and in the course of his novels he creates a coherent and
richly symbolic world which carries a major part of his thematic burden. At
the centre of this fictional world . . . is Britain, a country with moribund
tendencies which are powerfully expressed through images of darkness, de-
crepitude, emptiness and coldness. Description reveals the rest of Western
Europe to be in much the same condition, although at times a cold, efficient
sterility has replaced decay. In both cases descriptive passages are replete
with a sense of loss or absence that points to the superiority of the past.
Satisfactory alternatives to a Western Europe "grown old and cold and
weary" are not easily found. American landscapes appear to be bright and
spacious but are in reality meretricious, vulgar and militarist; Eastern European communist landscapes are even colder and darker than those of Western Europe and fail to make the faintest gesture towards something new.

East and West Europe and the United States are thus presented by
le Carré as dark places. The source of darkness, he suggests implicitly
throughout his novels and makes explicit in *The Naive and Sentimental
Lover*, is to be found in a loss of fundamental human values. Consequently,

From *The Novels of John le Carré: The Art of Survival.* © 1985 by David Monaghan.
Basil Blackwell, 1985.

only in his descriptions of Hong Kong—where despite the destructive influence of colonialism, Chinese culture retains values such as brotherly love and loyalty—does significant illumination enter le Carré's world. Le Carré is not, however, completely pessimistic about Western society, and he demonstrates on a number of occasions how quickly the individual who acts in a human way can restore light to the world. In *The Naive and Sentimental Lover,* Shamus, who strives to live in accordance with the demands of his feelings, and who makes love his most important value, is consistently associated with light. Jim Prideaux in *Tinker, Tailor, Soldier, Spy* and Mr Cardew in *A Murder of Quality* are other characters whose intrinsic humanity brightens the landscapes in which they are located.

I

Le Carré's descriptive techniques are most fully developed in his portrayal of Britain. Extensive detail plays a part in the creation of only a few of his British scenes and, with the exception of some of the more purple passages of his early fiction, he does not draw attention to their larger significance. However, through careful repetition of a certain set of characteristics, he is able to create a complex and symbolically charged landscape. Three of le Carré's longer passages of description, drawn from novels written at different stages of his career, should establish the main outlines of his British landscape. The first appears in *The Looking Glass War,* published in 1965, the second in *Tinker, Tailor, Soldier, Spy* (1974) and the third in *Smiley's People* (1980).

> The Department was housed in a crabbed, sooty villa of a place with a fire extinguisher on the balcony. It was like a house eternally for sale. No one knew why the Ministry put a wall round it; perhaps to protect it from the gaze of the people, like the wall round a cemetery; or the people from the gaze of the dead. Certainly not for the garden's sake, because nothing grew in it but grass which had worn away in patches like the coat of an old mongrel. The front door was painted dark green; it was never opened. By day anonymous vans of the same colour occasionally passed down the shabby drive, but they transacted their business in the back yard. . . . The building had that unmistakable air of controlled dilapidation which characterizes government hirings all over the world. For those who worked in it, its mystery was like the mystery of motherhood, its survival like the mystery of England.

Avery could remember it when the fog lingered contentedly against its stucco walls, or in the Summer, when the sunlight would briefly peer through the mesh curtains of his room, leaving no warmth, revealing no secrets. And he would remember it on that Winter dawn, its façade stained black, the street lights catching the raindrops on the grimy windows.

The lobby [of the Circus] looked dingier than ever. Three old lifts, a wooden barrier, a poster for Mazawattee tea, Bryant's glass-fronted sentry box with a Scenes of England calendar and a line of mossy telephones. . . .
    The grille of the centre lift rattled like a bunch of dry sticks. . . .
    The net curtained window [of the duty officers' room] looked onto a courtyard full of blackened pipes. . . . In the daytime the place was used as a restroom for girls with the vapours and to judge by the smell of cheap scent it still was. Along one wall lay the Rexine divan which at night made into a rotten bed; beside it the first-aid chest with the red cross peeling off the front, and a clapped-out television. . . . When he opened the door [of the steel cupboard] dust rolled out of the bottom in a cloud, crawled a distance then slowly lifted towards the dark window.

There are Victorian terraces in the region of Paddington Station that are painted as white as luxury liners on the outside, and inside are dark as tombs. Westbourne Terrace that Saturday morning gleamed as brightly as any of them, but the service road that led to Vladimir's part of it was blocked at one end by a heap of rotting mattresses, and by a smashed boom, like a frontier post, at the other. . . .
    Shedding chestnut trees darkened the pillared doorway, a scarred cat eyed him warily. The doorbell was the topmost of thirty but Smiley didn't press it and when he shoved the double doors they swung open too freely, revealing the same gloomy corridors painted very shiny to defeat graffiti writers, and the same linoleum staircase which squeaked like a hospital trolley. . . . There was no light switch and the stairs grew darker the higher he climbed. . . . There was a smell of too many people with not much money jammed into too little air.

Britain, as presented in these and numerous similar passages, is essentially urban and is filled with decaying ("rotting mattresses"; "mossy

telephones"), broken ("clapped-out television"; "smashed boom") and disintegrating ("the first-aid chest with the red cross peeling off the front";
"the building had that unmistakable air of controlled dilapidation") objects
and buildings. It is almost always dark ("dark window"; "trees darkened
the pillared doorway"; "the stairs grew darker") and there is little colour.
Only the green door of the Department and the white exterior of Westbourne
Terrace relieve the uniform blackness of the scenes quoted above ("sooty
villa"; "façade stained black"; "blackened pipes"; "gloomy corridors"). In
descriptions that appear elsewhere, black is often complemented by other
minimal colours such as grey, white, brown or a sickly yellow. Everything in
Britain appears to be dirty ("grimy windows"; "the lobby looked dingier
than ever") and the air is filled with dust ("dust rolled out of the bottom in
a cloud"). Most of le Carré's descriptions are characterized by a sense of
confinement and even entrapment ("a crabbed . . . villa"; "too many people
. . . jammed into too little air"). And yet at the same time his scenes are
often empty or deserted. The Department, "eternally for sale," seems about
to be abandoned, and in *Tinker, Tailor, Soldier, Spy* Smiley visits a wine bar,
"with music playing and no one there" and a pub with "the garden empty."

Recurring images of rot, dilapidation, dust, colourlessness and emptiness suggest that something is dead or dying. To reinforce the impression,
le Carré frequently introduces imagery associated with death and disease.
The wall around the Department is like "a wall round a cemetery"; the
insides of the Victorian terraces are "dark as tombs"; and the staircase
"squeaked like a hospital trolley." Similar metaphors are used throughout
le Carré's work. The slate roof of the Sawley Arms is coloured "the mauve
of half mourning"; "the row of villas which lines Western Avenue is like a
row of pink graves"; the music stands in Peter Worthington's room are
"crowded like skeletons into the corner of the room."

Not even nature, on those rare occasions when it intrudes into le Carré's
British landscape, offers any relief from the prevailing atmosphere of decay.
Fog and rain are the prevailing weather conditions ("the fog lingered contentedly"; "raindrops on the grimy windows") and when the sun does shine
it leaves "no warmth." The grass in the Department garden is "worn away
in patches like the coat of an old mongrel" and the chestnut trees on Westbourne Terrace are "shedding." Scenes set in the country possess no more
vitality. "The rain rolled like gun-smoke down the brown combes of the
Quantocks" as Prideaux drives to Thursgood's, and when Smiley walks on
the beach near Marazion "the day was grey, the seabirds were very white
against the slate sea." Similarly, the beech trees on Hampstead Heath "sank
away from [Smiley] like a retreating army in the mist. The darkness had

departed reluctantly, leaving an indoor gloom." The little sunlight which leaks through is "brown" and "burned like a slow bonfire in its own smoke."

By means of such descriptions le Carré creates a powerful and evocative, but obviously very selective landscape. Despite his reputation for working from photographs, le Carré's method is not photographic and he deliberately excludes a great deal to create his desired effect. Places that show no sign of deterioration are, for example, almost never described. The hairdresser's in Curzon Street, from which Smiley sees Martindale emerge, is identified only by the name Trumper's, because to do more would convey a visual message very different from le Carré's usual one. With its rich black marble and gold façade, its Royal crest and window display of old-fashioned, ivory-handled shaving equipment, Trumper's tells of an England still solid, wealthy and vigorously traditional.

What guides le Carré in creating his British landscape is a desire, not so much to describe the place as it is—which is not to deny that what he does describe has an authentic ring—but to provide visual equivalents for its spiritual and moral condition. British society and culture as a whole have grown "old and cold and weary" and are drawing close to, if they have not yet reached, death. This connection between landscape and the moribund state of the nation is made explicit by Peter Guillam's vision immediately prior to the unmasking of the mole Gerald: "he saw the whole architecture of that night in apocalyptic terms: the signals on the railway bridge turned to gallows, the Victorian warehouses to gigantic prisons, their windows barred and arched against the misty sky. Closer at hand, the ripple of rats and the stink of still water."

The British landscape created by le Carré possesses a temporal as well as spatial dimension which enables him to express not only what Britain has become but also what has been lost. His descriptions thus remind us that the shoddy and disintegrating world of contemporary Britain is the last phase of a long and frequently impressive history that he traces back to pre-Roman times: "The hills were olive and shaven, and had once been hill-forts." Le Carré achieves this historical perspective by focusing much of his description on places and buildings which, when they were created, embodied some of their society's major values and so now recall almost automatically their period of origin. The technique is firmly established in *A Murder of Quality*. King Arthur's Church, where, according to legend, Arthur paid homage to St Andrew, becomes an emblem of the post-Roman era when the dark age of myth gradually yielded to the light of Christianity. Carne Castle and Carne Abbey have similar symbolic implications: they stand for the joint aristocratic and ecclesiastical power upon which medieval society was founded.

The ways in which aristocratic power endured and evolved from the Renaissance to the end of the eighteenth century, as domestic and political arts replaced military ones, are represented by the fortified manor house, Haverdown, in *The Naive and Sentimental Lover,* and the "beautiful Palladian house," Millponds, in *Tinker, Tailor, Soldier, Spy.* It is, however, the Victorian and Edwardian eras that loom largest in le Carré's landscape. Carne, an ancient establishment, achieved full stature in this period. It stands as an emblem of the golden age of the public schools when, under the influence of Arnold's reforms at Rugby, they were largely responsible for producing a new type of morally earnest and Empire-minded ruling class. The great government buildings of London, most notably the Circus, recall the development of parliamentary democracy and the growth of a centralized bureaucracy. And the North Oxford house in *The Looking Glass War,* with its "pictures of some unknown family," its "palm cross" and "bible table" and its furniture "of mahogany, with brass inlay," is clearly a product of the Victorian bourgeois ideals of family, piety and solid materialism.

Enough is left of the original shape of these and other crumbling monuments to past greatness to provide the reader with a fairly precise picture of the values that are disappearing as Britain dies. What the architecture of the past suggests above all is that, at least up until the late nineteenth century, British society was infused with a sense of beauty, peace and order. The medieval Abbey Close at Carne is "serene and beautiful" and the two clockwork knights who perform a courtly ritual to mark the half hours on the Abbey clock establish a close relationship between social and aesthetic order: "the clock high above him struck the half-hour, and two knights on horseback rode out from their little castle over the door, and slowly raised their lances to each other in salute." Eighteenth-century buildings, such as the Georgian mansion in *Tinker, Tailor, Soldier, Spy,* possess similar qualities. The desire of the gambling club, which now occupies the premises, to lend an air of dignity to its proceedings makes this, ironically, one of the few well-preserved buildings in le Carré's novels and its original, elegant structure, based on contrasting circles and straight lines, is still very much in evidence: "There were five steps and a brass doorbell in a scalloped recess. The door was black with pillars either side. . . . He entered a circular hallway." Connie describes the now ruined Millponds as being "beautiful" with "lovely grounds," and the drawing room of Smiley's house in Bywater Street is "pretty" and "tall, with eighteenth-century mouldings, long windows and a good fireplace."

The beauty and harmony of these buildings is usually complemented by a sense of spaciousness and solidity, the whole effect contrasting sharply with the ugly, fragmented, cramped and flimsy nature of the modern landscape. Thus, under its presumably recent covering of "meagre coconut matting," the staircase at the Sawley Arms is "wide" and made of "marble." The North Oxford house is also "spacious" and its furniture is of mahogany and brass. Even more impressive in communicating a sense of space are Haverdown with its "interminable" corridors and "forty acres" of grounds and the Victorian terraces near Paddington Station, the sweep and scope of which le Carré likens to "luxury liners."

Also prominent in the historical periods to which le Carré alludes are objects and buildings created as expressions of the religious spirit. His novels include the early Christian King Arthur's Church, the medieval Carne Abbey, the bible desk in the Georgian mansion, the religious objects in the Victorian North Oxford house, and the possibly ancient but certainly pre-1920 parish church in Walliston. Their present condition clearly demonstrates that the spiritual impulse is part of what is dying in the modern world. King Arthur's Church is "empty, falling to bits"; the Abbey saints are "mutilated"; the bible desk holds the gambling club's membership book; and the parish church has been isolated by road development.

Just as le Carré's now disintegrating buildings were at one time graceful, harmonious and spacious, and were infused with a powerful spiritual quality, so there are signs that nature too was once a vital and life-enhancing force. Connie's photograph of Sarratt actually transports us into the past and, instead of the "sorry place" encountered by Smiley in *Tinker, Tailor, Soldier, Spy,* where "most of the elms had gone with the disease" and "pylons burgeoned over the old cricket field," we see "the grounds stretching out . . . mown and sunlit and the sight screens glistening." The countryside around the Sercomb family home in Cornwall acquires a temporal dimension through a series of implied contrasts between its present sterility and past fruitfulness. References to "a coppice of bare elms still waiting for the blight"; "stubs of felled trees"; "acres of smashed greenhouses"; "an untended kitchen garden"; "collapsed stables" contain powerful suggestions of a time when the trees thrived, the greenhouses and the garden nurtured growth, and horses occupied the stables. The existence of a gun room and a fishing room in the house further imply that the estate once supported wild as well as domestic animal life.

Modern buildings are relatively scarce in le Carré's British landscape and their nature as well as their number suggests the failure of attempts to revitalize the dying culture. These buildings fall into two categories: those which seek to revive past glories by imitating archaic styles and those which strive to express something new. The shoddiness, lack of imagination and spiritual poverty of modern Britain are equally evident in both. The first type not only demonstrate a lack of creative spirit but are also poor copies, substituting flimsy materials and mere decorative intentions for the solid and significant creations of the past. The medieval dungeon design of the Fleet Street "ground-floor cellar" bar with its "plastic prison arches" and "fake muskets" is typical in being both functionless and shoddy. Lacon's "Berkshire Camelot" operates on a grander scale but is equally pointless. "Stained-glass windows twenty feet high and a pine gallery over the entrance" seek to recreate the glories of a medieval manor but succeed only in making it "the ugliest house for miles around." The Police Station at Carne, "built ninety years ago to withstand the onslaughts of archery and battering rams," and the Fountain Café in suburban Walliston, "all Tudor and horse brasses," are further examples of the futility of attempts to use the past to dignify the present.

The emptiness of the modern spirit is more directly evident in the second type of building, of which the tower block in St John's Wood is perhaps the best example. In front there is "a large sculpture describing . . . nothing but a sort of cosmic muddle." The use of "terrazzo tile" and "a banister of African teak" on the stairs which Smiley descends demonstrates some concern with style and solidity, but it is one that lacks any hint of an authentic native voice. Further down even this is revealed to be a veneer aimed to cover the real cheapness and sordidness of the project: "Rough-rendered plaster replaced the earlier luxury and a stench of uncollected refuse crammed the air." Other dimensions of the modern spirit are revealed by the motel room in which Smiley meets Jim Prideaux. Its matching yellow and orange fittings attempt to supply the vitality and good taste usually lacking in le Carré's British landscape, but in fact simply deprive everything in the room of individual identity. Even the label on the vodka bottle merges into the overall colour scheme. But what is more striking than the room's lack of individual character is its insubstantiality. Materials such as marble, mahogany and brass play no part in the construction of this place and "the state of restlessness was constant. Even when the traffic outside went through one of its rare lulls the windows continued vibrating. In the bathroom the tooth glasses also vibrated, while from either wall and above them they could hear music, thumps and bits of conversation or laughter."

Le Carré's vision of a Britain caught between a decaying past and an empty, pointless present is epitomized by his description of the night of Haydon's capture. The Circus itself is not described, but it has been well established in earlier descriptions, such as the one quoted near the beginning of this chapter, as a rotting monument to the glory of British government institutions. Close to it are a number of shoddy buildings that strive for dignity by imitating aspects of the past: "the buildings were gimcrack, cheaply fitted out with bits of empire: a Roman bank, a theatre like a vast desecrated mosque." And in the background, advancing "like an army of robots," are the "highrise blocks" which for le Carré are the most authentic expression of the absence from modern Britain of significant imaginative and spiritual qualities.

II

Le Carré's Western European landscapes share many of the characteristics of his British ones. They are typically colourless, flat, dingy and incomplete and are usually shrouded in snow, rain or fog. As such they also communicate a sense of moral and spiritual *malaise,* an effect that le Carré again heightens by his use of death imagery. Finland, in *The Looking Glass War,* is particularly corpse-like. Snow and mist cover everything and objects, "drained of colour, black carrion on a white desert," possess "no depth, no recession and no shadows." Figures and buildings are "locked in the cold like bodies in an icefloe." Bonn is almost as bleak. The weather is persistently foggy and wet and its flat grey-white landscape is scarred with incomplete ("giant buildings, still unfinished") or fractured ("one hill . . . is broken like a quarry") objects. An atmosphere of death is pervasive. Farmhouses and new building estates look like "hulks left over by the sea" and the Bundestag is "a vast motel mourned by its own flags."

Other German cities possess characteristics similar to Bonn's. As Leamas waits near the Berlin Wall he sees "empty" streets, and feels "the icy October wind." The Wall itself is "a dirty, ugly thing of breeze blocks and strands of barbed wire, lit with cheap yellow light." Smiley also experiences a "half-world of ruin" when, years later, he visits the Turkish quarter adjacent to the Wall to prepare for his final rendezvous with Karla. It is snowing and ferociously cold, and everything around him is either defunct ("the railway viaduct . . . was derelict, and no trains ever crossed"), decaying ("the shelter stank of leaf-mould and damp") or dead ("the warehouses . . . stood monstrous as the hulks of an earlier barbaric civilisation"). The Olympic Village in Munich, although the product of a much more hopeful spirit, is in no better condition than the Berlin Wall: "The Village is not a village at all, of course, but a marooned and disintegrating citadel of grey concrete." The staircase leading up to Kurtz's apartment there is "filthy" and the apartment itself "awfully down-at-heel" with windows that offer a "grimy view of the road to Dachau." The other Munich apartment occupied by the Israelis is "pervaded with an air of sad neglect" which creates "a mood of bereavement."

Le Carré's German landscapes often possess an historical dimension which suggests as clearly as do the British the superiority of the past. Repeated reminders that the hills around Bonn were "the land of the Nibelungs" and that the Drachenfels is "where Siegfried had slain the dragon and bathed in its magic blood" serve, for example, to establish a sharp contrast between the courage, purposefulness and vitality of the German heroic age, and the aimless time-serving that characterizes modern Bonn. However, this division between past and present, le Carré suggests in his descriptions of Dresden and Hamburg, is even more marked than in Britain because of the wholesale destruction and rebuilding which resulted from wartime bombing. Prewar Dresden is emblematic of much of what was best in the German past: Smiley "had loved its architecture, its odd jumble of medieval and classical buildings, sometimes reminiscent of Oxford, its cupolas, towers and spires, its copper-green roofs shimmering under a hot sun." The Second World War not only obliterates all this but, by stranding Dresden in the eastern part of a divided Germany, commits its future to a communist ideology that is completely alien to the spirit of individuality, creativity and spirituality so powerfully present in its past. Even though it remains in the West, the contrast between the pre- and postwar cities of Hamburg is almost as great. Reduced by war to "one endless smouldering bomb-site," Hamburg has been reborn as a place "hurtling into the anonymity of canned music, high-rise concrete and smoked glass." Thus, the "ancient, free, and Hanseatic City" which Smiley remembers from his youth as "a rich and graceful shipping town" is "now almost pounded to death by the thunder of its own prosperity."

The differences between contemporary Europe, particularly Germany, with its expensive but sterile landscapes created by the post-war rebuilding process and Britain, with its rotting remnants of former greatness, are epitomized by two descriptions of places dedicated to the sale of sex. The Pussywillow Club in Soho which Leamas visits in *The Spy Who Came In from the Cold* is located down "a narrow alley, at the far end of which shone a tawdry neon sign." Music is provided by a "two-piece band" which produces a "subdued moan," and the stripper is "a young, drab girl with a dark bruise on her thigh. She had that pitiful, spindly nakedness which is embarrassing because it is not erotic." The Blue Diamond Club in Hamburg is also to be found in an alley, but otherwise is very different. The anteroom is "trim" and "filled with grey machinery manned by a smart young man in a grey suit." On the desk there is "an elaborate telephone system." Doors open electronically to reveal girls who are "beautiful, naked and young." The manager's office is "clean as a doctor's surgery with a polished plastic desk and a lot more machinery."

No healthy human impulse or real vitality is to be found in either place. The Soho stripper is not erotic and Smiley finds the "demonstration of love-making" staged at the Blue Diamond "mechanical, pointless, dispiriting." However, the British setting does at least hint at some former energy now drained away. Feeble though it may be, the music is still produced by people, thereby connecting it, if only remotely, to one of the most significant of the human creative acts. Similarly, the stripper may be bruised, but this at least affirms that she is flesh and blood and distantly related to an ideal of whole and fecund female beauty and sexuality. The Blue Diamond, on the other hand, with its emphasis on efficiency, technology and profit, is completely divorced from the finer human urges and bears no relationship whatsoever to the spirit that lies behind the myths of the *Nibelungen* or the old city of Dresden.

As was the case with British architecture such as the St John's Wood tower block, but on a much larger scale, European efforts to create something new thus reveal nothing more than the poverty of the modern spirit. That there is some recognition of this is made evident by occasional attempts to shape contemporary buildings along traditional lines. However, as with similar efforts in Britain, these anachronistic creations fail completely to recapture any of the glories of the past and serve only to reinforce our sense of the inferiority of the present. This is true, for instance, of the motel outside Munich which "had been built twelve months ago for medievally-minded lovers, with cement-stippled cloisters, plastic muskets, and tinted neon lighting."

Le Carré makes his point most tellingly by juxtaposing descriptions of the Bellevue Palace Hotel in Bern and the café-restaurant in Thun. The former is a rare example of something old that retains its original grandeur. It is "an enormous, sumptuous place of mellowed Edwardian quiet" and Smiley's room is "a tiny Swiss Versailles. The *bombé* writing-desk had brass inlay and a marble top, a Bartlett print of Lord Byron's Childe Harold hung above the pristine twin beds." The café, which le Carré describes as "modern Swiss antique," offers nothing more than a pathetic parody of the values the hotel represents. Where the Bellevue Palace employs materials that demonstrate a concern for beauty and durability, the café has "stucco pillars" on which hang "plastic lances." Similarly, the integration of function and form evident in the writing desk with its brass inlay and marble top has been replaced by the merely decorative: "The lamps were wrought iron but the illumination came from a ring of strip lighting round the ceiling." Finally, the values of generosity and hospitality suggested by the adjectives "enormous," "sumptuous" and "mellowed" have diminished into the stingy and grudging attitude epitomized by the waitress who denies Smiley's request that his *café-crème* be served in a glass.

Through description, then, le Carré offers us a vision of the decline of the major Western European nations. Images of social harmony, aesthetic wholeness and cultural and spiritual vitality all belong to the past and the modern world is characterized either by decay or by sterile and mechanical innovation. However, if we broaden le Carré's canvas to include communist-bloc and American landscapes we can see that he finds little that is appealing in the alternatives that lie to the East or to the West.

III

None of le Carré's novels is set in the United States, but a number of scenes take place in American embassies and military bases and these provide the basis for the creation of a sketchily defined but evocative landscape. At first sight, this American landscape with its *"dimension,"* "optimism" and dazzling illumination ("the American Embassy, brilliant as a power house, drove yellow shafts through the mist") offers an attractive alternative to the constricted and dark vistas of Western Europe. There is, for example, a marked contrast between the entertainment facilities of British and American intelligence. Whereas the British provide hospitality in a gutted Circus, serving drinks from "a trestle table" with "a darned damask tablecloth spread over it," the Americans have a "vast rooftop bar, known within the Circus as the planetarium," which provides superb views across London. However, the sense of vision proves to be false, the brilliance illusory and the optimism ill-founded. Martello's office is impressive because of its size, but it is finally more significant that the rosewood table is "fake," and that the room is furnished with "airline chairs" and an "empty" desk. As these images suggest, the Americans lack any authentic vision or sense of personal identity with which to fill their territory. All they have to offer is a shallow patriotism symbolized by the flag and the Presidential portraits to be found in both Martello's office and the American Embassy in Hong Kong. As a result the feeling of spaciousness is quickly transformed into one of arid bareness.

In a sense, le Carré's Americans are a pathetic people whose brilliance reveals nothing but their own emptiness. However, he has little pity to spare for them because out of their unthinking patriotism springs the conviction that it is justifiable to use arms to propagate the American way of life. During

Westerby's swing through the Asian war zone, we are given repeated glimpses of the disastrous consequences of the Americans' stupid assumption that they have a right to impose a set of values characterized by a jumble of messages about "higher education," "cut-price washing machines" and "prayer" on other cultures. Enclosed behind "smoked glass" windows, in "soundproof" rooms which, with their "fake fireplace[s]" and "Andrew Wyeth reproduction[s]" fail to make any concession to the local environment, the American military is completely unequipped to recognize that "electronics base[s]" dumped in the midst of paddie fields are inadequate compensation for the destruction of a vibrant and at times magical culture: "From the river thirty feet below them came the murmured chant of the sampans as they drifted like long leaves across the golden moon-path. From the sky . . . came the occasional ragged flashes of outgoing gunfire." For le Carré, a society which is willing to replace this "golden moon-path" with "a single infernal light, like the promise of a future war" has little to offer as an alternative even to the most decadent of the older democracies. In the final analysis, the light the Americans emit not only exposes their hollowness, it also blinds the viewer to their ugliness. At night the American aircraft carrier makes a brave show in Hong Kong harbour, where "floodlit and dressed overall, [it] basked like a pampered woman amid a cluster of attendant launches." Viewed in daylight it proves to be "grey and menacing, like an unsheathed knife." Similarly the lights that suddenly brighten the sky above Po Toi during the festival of Tin Hau, prove not to be a means of revealing the godhead but of "blinding" those below to the presence of "blackened [American] helicopters" on a mission of slaughter.

Communist Europe is, however, even less appealing than the United States, and le Carré's descriptions of East Germany are the ugliest, bleakest and most despairing of any that appear in his novels. To some extent East Germany simply shares the *malaise* from which Britain and Western Europe suffer. Its landscapes, both urban and rural, are characterized by the same lack of colour, the same darkness, emptiness, sense of disintegration and decay, and continual rain as those to the West. The Church tower in Kalkstadt is "black and empty"; Leiser's room in the town is "large and bare," with walls of "grey plaster" over which "the damp had spread . . . in dark shadows." The street lights close to the Berlin Wall are "dingy," the market stalls "empty." A fence is "broken" and a building "windowless." Empty doorways "gaped sightlessly" and the Wall itself is "grey-brown in the weary arclight." Alec Leamas passes through this despairing scene in the rain and "pitch dark." The Peace Hall in Leipzig is made of "pre-cast concrete with . . . cracks in the corners" and is decorated with "dusty" bunting which "looked like something from a fascist funeral." Rural scenes are no less drab and sterile: "The steep wooded hills on either side gradually yielded their colours to the gathering dusk until they stood grey and lifeless in the twilight."

Significant colour appears only once in all of le Carré's Eastern European scenes. In the secret courtroom where Leamas is exposed as a double agent, red stands out in sharp contrast to the otherwise unremitting shades of black and grey: "Above them, suspended from the ceiling by three loops of wire, was a large red star made of plywood." However, since the star is the symbol of the communist absolutism responsible for the bleak and colourless landscape over which it presides, the use of colour here is clearly ironic. Light is employed towards similarly ironic ends on the one occasion that it penetrates the all-pervading gloom. As is the case with the American helicopter in *The Honourable Schoolboy*, the searchlights that play on the Berlin Wall during Leamas's attempt to escape blind rather than illuminate and are harbingers of death rather than revelation:

> Suddenly the whole world seemed to break into flame; from everywhere, from above and beside them, massive lights converged, bursting upon them with savage accuracy.
>
> Leamas was blinded. . . . He could see nothing—only a mad confusion of colour dancing in his eyes.
>
> Shielding his eyes he looked down at the foot of the wall and at last he managed to see her, lying still. . . . She was dead.
>
> Finally they shot him, two or three shots. He stood glaring round him like a blinded bull in the arena.

Eastern Europe is, finally, the most desolate of all le Carré's landscapes because it does not contain even the hint of a desire to find something new with which to replace the crumbling fragments of a defunct culture. As Leiser travels across East Germany he observes all around him decay and destruction: "The house was old, falling with neglect; the drive overgrown with grass, pitted with cart tracks. The fences were broken." But what strikes him most is the complete lack of interest in doing anything to halt the process of disintegration: "There were no signposts and no new buildings, it suddenly occurred to him. That was where the peace came from, it was the peace of no innovation—it might have been fifty years ago, a hundred. . . . It was the darkness of indifference." The spirit of "innovation" responsible for the terrazzo tile and African teak banisters in the St John's Wood tower block does not lead to happy results. Nevertheless, it does demonstrate that in Britain the will to make things new still exists, if only feebly. By contrast there is such a profound indifference in East Germany that anything new which is built, such as the block of workers' flats in Kalkstadt, is simply designed to conform to the prevailing grey drabness. Everything about these flats, from their "shoddy walls" and location on "a patch of waste land," to the failure to give them a name, demonstrates a total lack of the creative impulse. Consequently, the atmosphere which emanates from the place is one that we would associate usually with something close to death rather than newly born: "Pale lights shone in almost every window; six floors. Stone steps, thick with leaves, led to the cellar. . . . The first room was large and airless."

IV

Le Carré's landscapes define the modern world as a dark place, lacking moral or spiritual illumination. However, if we explore this use of dark and light as an aspect of description a little further, we can see that le Carré's pessimism is not absolute, and that he is willing to suggest ways in which the death of modern civilization can be prevented. Such a study must take as its starting point an examination of the role of Hong Kong in the novelist's world landscape.

To a certain extent le Carré employs Hong Kong in *The Honourable Schoolboy* as a part of his analysis of the decline of British society, for even as it is sinking into its own deathbed, Britain has reached out a palsied arm and presumed to infect another culture with its disease. Displaying insensitivity to the authenticity of other ways of life almost equal to that of the Americans in Vietnam and Cambodia, the British colonialists have imposed on Hong Kong a network of their own sterile customs. The tedious rituals of the Foreign Correspondents' Club, the dull cricket games played by the "Peak mafia," and race-track presentations modelled on prize-giving ceremonies at English village fêtes make Hong Kong society seem almost as lifeless as that in Britain. Even worse the mixture of incompatible cultures which results from the British presence often has ludicrous results, as, for example, in "the Tudor pub in the unfinished high-rise building" and the "rooftop bar . . . with its four-piece Chinese band playing Noël Coward, and its straight-faced Chinese barmen in periwigs and frock-coats."

However, Hong Kong functions as more than a symbol of the destructive effects of colonialism, for it also possesses a vitality, energy, beauty and quality of illumination rarely found in le Carré's novels. The following descriptions are typical: "Behind the black Peak a full moon, not yet risen, glowed like a forest fire"; "the harbour lay like a perfect mirror at the centre of the jewel box"; "Behind him hung the Peak, its shoulders festooned in gold lights." The source of this beauty and light is to be found in the ability of the Chinese, at some fundamental level, to resist the taint of British influence. Westerby is acutely conscious that in essentials, Chinese society is completely hidden from the "roundeye" who "could live all his life in the same block and never have the smallest notion of the secret tic-tac on his doorstep." After twenty-five years in the East, he finds it as "obscure" as ever. Thus, when the Chinese go about their own business they do so in a spirit very different from the British, and there is a sharp contrast, for instance, between life on the roof-tops and on the cricket field. Whereas the one is "a breathtaking theatre of survival" embodying sweat-shops, religious services, mah-jong games, fortune telling and schools for "dancing, reading, ballet, recreation and combat," the other involves "fifteen whiteclad figures" who "lounged" "on a patch of perfect English lawn" at the beginning of "a long dull innings to no applause."

The Chinese direct their energy, as the roof-top scene suggests, towards a rich variety of objects, ranging from the grossly materialistic to the deeply spiritual. However, for le Carré, the society's vitality is rooted in the ability of its members to remain committed to some fundamental human concerns of which the British have, by and large, lost sight. Drake Ko, le Carré's only fully developed Chinese character, is an entrepreneur and a quasi-gangster, who will kill if crossed. Yet his behaviour is rooted in a consistent moral system that demands complete loyalty to family, clan and those with whom he has created a bond of trust. For Ko, one must "hold fast to that which is good. . . . That is what God likes" and the chance of reunion with a brother whom he "loved" justifies risking everything. Thus, Lizzie Worthington, the only British character who comes close to understanding Ko, is anxious, above all, to convince him that, "I kept faith. . . . I stuck to the deal" because "it's what he cares about most."

There is, therefore, a direct relationship between the presence of light in le Carré's Hong Kong landscape and the society's ability to retain contact with those basic human urges defined in chapter 1. How Western societies are to follow the example set by Hong Kong and escape their prevailing darkness is a problem to which le Carré provides no ready answers. However, through a number of scenes in which landscape is related to character rather than country, he does suggest that the beginnings of a solution lie within the power of each of us; by maintaining or regaining contact with the instinctual bases of personality any individual can restore some value or light to the world. Carne, one of the most sterile places in all of le Carré's novels, is, for example, briefly transformed under the influence of Mr Cardew, a man of spiritual insight and personal warmth. His Tabernacle is not cheap, crumbling or dirty but is a place of "thickly-varnished ochre pine" and an active "polishing" of "the heavy brass chandelier." To one side, there is "a small vegetable garden, carefully tilled, with bright yellow paths running between the empty beds." Mr Cardew has created an oasis within the modern desert and it is apt that on the day Smiley visits him, instead of the usual rain and gloom, "the sun shone through the crisp air. It was a cold, beautiful day."

A similar relationship is established between landscape and character during the episode when Smiley questions Jim Prideaux. For all his limitations, Prideaux is fundamentally a good human being motivated by love for his fellow men and for his country. These qualities shine through his account of the otherwise sordid Operation Testify. As Jim's story gets under way and his naive vision begins to make itself felt, it is appropriate that he and Smiley move out of the confined, cheap and restless motel and to "a hilltop free of fog." Here a "long view" is possible, "scattered lights reached into the distance," "the sky was light," and "the stars were very clear." In contrast to the night of Operation Testify when there was "no moon," on this occasion "the half moon was free of cloud." Under Prideaux's influence the landscape is, albeit only temporarily, transformed: "The night landscape seemed to Smiley suddenly innocent; it was like a great canvas on which nothing bad or cruel had ever been painted."

This ability of the individual to reintroduce light into the world is explored most fully and most explicitly in *The Naive and Sentimental Lover*. Shamus's determination to live in accordance with the dictates of his feelings and to pursue the ideal of love is defined quite specifically as a search for light and a rejection of darkness: "We don't want *all right,* do we, lover. . . . Never did, never will. We want the sun, not the fucking twilight." Similarly, Helen comments that Shamus is fighting "greyness" and defines Cassidy's final failure to put a value on himself, as going "back into that awful dark."

The effect that an individual such as Shamus can have on a dying culture becomes evident during Cassidy's visit to Haverdown. Haverdown itself is one of le Carré's clearest symbols of the decline of Britain. Begun in the thirteenth century its architecture reflects the main stages in English history [through] the Georgian period. Today, however, it is neglected and in decay, a process le Carré emphasizes through ironic contrasts between the estate agent's idealized description of the place and the modern actuality: "*The entrance is marked by a Pair of finely pointed stone gateposts surmounted by ornamental Beasts dating from the sixteenth Century.* Directly before him, two disintegrating griffins, glumly clutching armorial shields, rose into the green darkness of a beech tree." What Cassidy sees as he views Haverdown in "twilight" is "the hulk of a dozen English generations," and just as the light is "dying," so, it seems, is Britain.

However, the elegiac tone which has pervaded the scene up to this point is broken when "a real light" suddenly penetrates the gloom, announcing the arrival of Shamus. At first Shamus's features are hidden by the glow of the lamp and so for Cassidy, Shamus's identity is entirely bound up in the light. When Shamus answers a question, it seems to Cassidy that "the lantern replied." This identification of Shamus with light is further intensified by the way in which his face is eventually revealed to Cassidy: "In the same moment a ray of red sunlight, reflected from the upper window of the chapel, broke like a tiny dawn over the interior of the porch and provided Cassidy with a first sight of his examiner." From here on until the souring of their relationship as a consequence of Cassidy's affair with Helen, Shamus consistently brightens the gloomy modern world for Cassidy. Cassidy's experience of "standing in the total blackness of an unknown interior with only his host's friendly grasp to guide him" reminds him of waiting in the cinema for the "grey rectangle" to be drawn back and the brilliantly lit screen to be revealed. However, whereas cinematic light produces only "hallucinations," Shamus offers genuine enlightenment.

Shamus assumes his role as Cassidy's guide during this first evening. By keeping control of the lantern while showing Cassidy over the house, he is the source of what little illumination is possible in this dark and dying place. At the end of the tour his lantern, assisted by the firelight, provides Cassidy with his first view of Helen. So "utterly improbable" is this fleeting vision of naked beauty that Cassidy might have dismissed it as an illusion "had not the beam of the lantern firmly pointed him the proof of her terrestrial existence." As Shamus's influence grows, so it seems the world responds by becoming lighter: "shoulder to shoulder" during their "pee-break," Shamus and Cassidy view the night in its "alpine majesty" and see the house rise "in countless peaks against the pale sky, where powdery swarms of stars followed the moonlit ridges of the clouds like fireflies frozen into the external ice. At their feet a white dew glistened." It is, as Shamus comments, quoting Joyce, "the heaventree of stars. . . . Hung with humid nightree fruit," that Cassidy is seeing for the first time. Later in the evening Shamus takes Cassidy to a pub "higher up the hill . . . a leafy place with a verandah and a long view of the valley lights. The lights reached to the edge of the earth, melting together in a low haze of gold before joining the descending stars." The night light is equally magical during Shamus and Cassidy's "love affair" in Paris: "Diamonds surrounded them: hung in giant clusters in the window panes, pricked the orange night sky, were draped in the eyes of lovers and in the brown silk of women's hair." On the first day of this same trip, Cassidy experiences the even more brilliant illumination of the sun: Paris is "bathed in perfect sunlight. It fired the river, shimmered in the pink streets, and turned the golden eagles into phoenixes of present joy."

The light created by Cassidy and Shamus's relationship, in which for a while "one perfect summer's day followed another," eventually fades and, in the climactic alpine scenes, the landscape emanates once again an atmosphere of death. Indeed, the snow that falls and covers everything as Cassidy betrays his commitment to Helen comes close to suggesting, as it does in the similar scene with which Joyce ends "The Dead," the inevitable annihilation of all life:

> The snow had almost covered them. Sometimes he saw them, sometimes there was nothing; it was no longer possible to tell. Once, through a clearing as it were, he made out two uprights, one straight and one crooked, and either they were posts along the fencing or two people leaning together as they struggled with the very deep snow. But . . . they vanished finally, into the nothing that lay beyond the blizzard.

Like Prideaux, Shamus is therefore unable to make the world innocent for very long; the efforts of both men are nonetheless significant, for they demonstrate that redemption is possible. Given the dreadful bleakness of landscapes stripped of the force of love, it seems inevitable that there will be other occasions upon which the naive spirit will assert itself.

A study of le Carré's landscapes leaves the reader face to face once again with the paradoxes that lie at the centre of his vision. As a social critic he presents powerful metaphors for a world that has lost its vital spark and is dying, and nothing the individual can do seems likely to reverse this process. And yet, as a romantic, le Carré attaches great significance to any life-affirming gesture, and is ever ready to celebrate those occasions, however fleeting, on which one of his characters is able to infuse a dreary landscape with glorious light.

SUSAN LAITY

"The Second Burden of a Former Child": Doubling and Repetition in A Perfect Spy

If there be nothing new but that which is
Hath been before, how are our brains beguiled,
Which laboring for invention, bear amiss
The second burden of a former child!
—WILLIAM SHAKESPEARE, Sonnet 59

In 1968, John le Carré wrote an introduction to Bruce Page, David Leitch, and Philip Knightley's book *Philby: The Spy Who Betrayed a Generation,* in which he declared that "like a great novel, and an unfinished one at that, the story of Kim Philby lives on in us." And indeed, if we examine le Carré's own fiction, we see *his* story, at least, of Kim Philby living on in endless repetition. For the fifteen pages that comprise le Carré's introduction to *Philby* contain as well the tale of his spy fiction; make up, in effect, a schema for such later books as *Tinker, Tailor, Soldier, Spy, The Little Drummer Girl,* and, especially, *A Perfect Spy.* Here are the familiar themes: the secret world as a microcosm of, and a commentary on, contemporary British society; the complicity of the betrayed with the betrayal; the betrayer as "one of us" even as he is one of them. Here, in the story of Britain's most famous (and infamous) double agent, le Carré finds a matrix for his own world of double agents, doubles, reduplication, and repetition; in his compulsion to retell that story, I shall argue, he seeks what Nietzsche calls in *Thus Spake Zarathustra* the will's revenge against time and time's "'It was.'"

Double agents have always been prominent in le Carré's fiction: *Tinker,*

Tailor, Soldier, Spy involves the search for the mole Gerald; Charlie, in *The Little Drummer Girl,* is sent to penetrate a Palestinian terrorist group; Mundt, in *The Spy Who Came In from the Cold,* and Nelson Ko, in *The Honourable Schoolboy,* are both moles in place. In addition, *Call for the Dead* and *A Small Town in Germany* appear for a major portion of their texts to involve investigations into double agents, only to reverse themselves and end with the unmasking of the supposed traitors as agents acting out of loyalty to Western interests: Samuel Fennan was preparing to expose his wife as an enemy (not double) agent; Leo Harting was pursuing a Nazi war criminal—against what turn out to be the real British sympathies, it is true, but honoring their expressed wishes. I have chosen to concentrate on *A Perfect Spy* in part because it deals specifically with a double agent, although I do not feel that the double agent figure *per se* carries the resonances normally to be found in the literature of doubling. Rather, I shall argue, le Carré uses his agents as doubles: metaphors for a world divided against itself; a world in which men must constantly struggle to discriminate among conflicting loyalties and shifting identities. His creation of those doubles, I shall further argue, as well as the repetitions to be found not only within *A Perfect Spy* but also between texts, both invoke the psychic resonances considered by Freud, Rank, and Nietzsche, and are themselves a kind of doubling, of author in text and author and text, with which le Carré wills his own redemption against the "it was" of time. Before I look at the book, however, I should like briefly to consider the term *double agent* and its applicability within the fiction of le Carré.

In his complacent narrative of some twenty-five years of treason, *My Silent War,* Kim Philby takes up the question of whether he was a double agent:

> Some writers have recently spoken of me as a double agent, or even as a triple agent. If this is taken to mean that I was working with equal zeal for two or more sides at once, it is seriously misleading. All through my career, I have been a straight penetration agent working in the Soviet interest. The fact that I joined the British Secret Intelligence Service is neither here nor there; I regarded my SIS appointments purely in the light of cover-jobs, to be carried out sufficiently well to ensure my attaining positions in which my service to the Soviet Union would be most effective. My connection with SIS must be seen against my prior total commitment to the Soviet Union.

Despite his specious argument that being director of anti-Soviet operations for M.I.6 is merely a cover job, roughly equivalent to being, say, a vacuum cleaner salesman, Philby makes an important point here. Frequently in spy fiction characters are referred to as "double agents" who are, in fact, "straight penetration agents." Indeed, le Carré makes classifying Bill Haydon, Charlie, and especially Magnus Pym deliberately difficult. (Neither Mundt nor Nelson Ko presents the same ambiguity; Mundt's position is merely a fact which we don't know until the end of the book, while Nelson is too distant a character—we are concerned with how people respond *to him,* not with his own responses.) Bill Haydon, who at first seems to be solely a Soviet agent, tells Smiley different versions of his recruitment—its date and its impact—so that, while by the time of *Tinker, Tailor* his loyalties (or at least his masters) are clearly Soviet, nonetheless a very real possibility remains that he was originally a British, and then a true double, agent. Charlie is recruited by the Israelis to lead them to a Palestinian terrorist, but she herself remains in ignorance for much of the novel of her mission; after she joins the Palestinians in Lebanon, her loyalties are sharply divided—so much so that no one is quite sure *whom* she is working for. And Pym— what are his loyalties? He is recruited practically simultaneously by Brotherhood and Axel/Poppy; his first act as Brotherhood's agent is unthinkingly to betray Axel, while his later loyalties are given wholly to Axel, but never, it seems, to Axel's superiors, whoever they may be. As a working term, I intend to use *double agent* to refer to someone employed simultaneously by two opposed secret services; but the ambiguity of the term, and the ambivalence of the agent who earns it, must be borne in mind.

Doubling in *A Perfect Spy* goes far beyond the bounds of mere double agents, or simply the opposition inherent in the "us" and "them" nature of the spy story. Certainly there are the primary doubles: the British Secret Service versus the Czech Service, and versus, for that matter, the American Service; and Pym's two agent runners, Brotherhood and Poppy, but there are in addition so many doubles, such prolific reduplication, that the book takes on an almost incestuous quality of perpetual renewal. A brief resumé of some of the doubled characters, both major and minor, will give us some sense of the depth of the book's obsession.

Brotherhood and Axel/Poppy, Pym's two masters, have more in common than their similar roles—le Carré clearly means them to be seen as Pym's alternate fathers. Physically alike (Tom describes Poppy's shaggy eyebrows as being like Jack's), the same age, both have been in the war and both have suffered there—Brotherhood's arm is mangled, Poppy limps. Their war experiences give them what Pym describes as "crucial years" on him. At the same time, they are clearly mirrored doubles—opposite numbers in more important ways than politics. As Pym rejoices after his visit with Brotherhood:

> In a single Christmas, God had dished him up two saints. The one was on the run and couldn't walk, the other was a handsome English warlord who served sherry on Boxing Day and had never had a doubt in his life. Both admired him, both loved his jokes and his voices, both were clamouring to occupy the empty spaces of his heart. In return he was giving to each man the character he seemed to be in search of.

Indeed, the whole history of Pym's encounter with Jack and Poppy in Bern is the story of a dual relationship: with one man who does not understand Pym at all and one who comprehends him instantly; who together appeal to the two halves of Pym's head, and who together replace the absent Rick.

That each is meant to be a father for Pym, and thus is a double for Rick is stated explicitly and frequently throughout the text; Sefton Boyd tells Brotherhood that when Pym called to make a drunken confession (to carving Sefton Boyd's initials on a lavatory wall, some thirty-five years earlier), he "said there was this Englishman he worked for, called him the Brotherhood. . . . There was the Brotherhood and there was this other chap. Said he was working for both of 'em. They were like two parents for him. Kept him going." Poppy is also, however, Pym's Wentworth, his nemesis as Wentworth is Rick's; Brotherhood is also Tom's Uncle Jack, Pym's double, who passed on his mistress, Mary, to be Pym's wife—with Poppy's full approval. And Mary, making her first contact with Poppy, realizes he is "'the other half of Magnus, and therefore the other half of me.'" (Axel is, of course, also doubled by the two names he is finally known by—"Axel" and "Poppy" [Pop?], which is taken at first to be a woman's name and then turns out to be Axel's code name, a reference to the Flanders poppy.)

As Pym has fathers who are also doubles, so he has a son, Tom, who copies Pym's walk, spies on his parents, and writes ardent letters to Becky Lederer although he prefers one of the Bursar's daughters, just as Pym wrote to Belinda while preferring Jemima. Pym has wives—two of them. His wedding to Belinda "received the Firm's approval while it still awaited his"; as for Mary, "Pym, with both his mentors pushing in the same direction, followed their advice and took Mary . . . to be his truly wedded partner at the High Table of the Anglo-American alliance. And really, after all that he had given away already, it seemed a very reasonable sacrifice." Mary, as well, was a spy, a pupil of Brotherhood's, as Pym was, and she exhibits considerable evasive tradecraft at the end of the novel, similar to Pym's maneuvers in slipping away at the beginning of the book.

To continue the familial doubling, Rick, reborn in Brotherhood and Axel, is himself the true son to his father-in-law, Makepeace Watermaster; he shows this in stealing Makepeace's inspirational speech about the stars, as he has earlier stolen his daughter, the woman Makepeace had desired. And Makepeace's home, The Glades, is Purgatory to Rick's Paradise, where Pym and his mother Dorothy suffer as fellow prisoners after the Fall.

Dorothy, Pym's blood mother, is doubled many times over, most importantly by the refugee Lippsie, who shares Rick's bed with Dorothy, and sees to Pym's care and education. There is also Cherry, Sefton Boyd's aunt, who is one of Rick's lovers and supporters until Pym tells her about Lippsie's charms. Also in Pym's childhood are the innumerable, faceless Mothers and Lovelies, there to perform Dorothy's maternal and connubial functions for Pym and Rick (who shall be reduplicated in the Marthas who serve Axel and the Michaels who are Pym's contacts). Later, in Bern, Frau Ollinger is the mother of what will be for Pym "a truly happy family"—the only one he meets. Finally, Mary is not only Pym's wife, she is Tom's mother; one of Pym's greatest pleasures is watching her ministering to their child.

Lippsie, Pym's other mother, reappears as both victim in Peggy Wentworth and Poppy (who reacquaints Pym with Lippsie's German Muse), and collaborator in conspiracy, again in Poppy/Axel, but also in such desirable women as E. Weber, Marlene, and Sabina.

Finally among the important double figures is Lederer, the American agent. Like Jack, Lederer tracks Pym, insisting on proclaiming his guilt despite pressure to keep quiet. But he is also like Pym; at the British/American conference, he muses on their similarities:

> What I recognize in Pym is what I recognize in myself: a spirit so wayward that, even while I am playing a game of Scrabble with my kids it can swing between the options of suicide, rape and assassination. "He's one of *us,* for Christ's sake!" Lederer wants to scream at the sleeping potentates around him. "Not one of you. One of *me.* We're howling psychopaths, the both of us."

Like Pym, as well, he is not above lying to his wife to keep his image going. He is, however, another mirrored double: while Lederer is always "seeing everything with perfect vision and being repeatedly dismissed as an unwelcome prophet," Pym has managed to systematically lie throughout his espionage career and be believed, even when his information is doubted.

Doubling is so obsessive in *A Perfect Spy* that even a minor character like Morrie Washington tries to get in on the act: "Morrie, though a third Rick's size, spends most of his life and all his money in an effort to achieve Total Assumption with his idol." Even then, doubling by duplication only covers one kind of twinning in the book; *A Perfect Spy* is equally concerned with the division within the self, the two or more versions of a person which live in one body.

We can confine ourselves here to the two people who most completely carry too many different selves within them: Rick and Pym. While le Carré refers to other divided people—for example, the bisexual/incestuous brother and sister, Kenneth and Jemima Sefton Boyd—he confines his most thorough explorations to the two elusive central figures. Indeed, as I shall discuss later in this essay, just as Brotherhood, Mary, and Lederer search for Pym, so Pym tries to discover himself, looking first for Rick as a path to Tom's father.

From the first, we are shown Rick's complex nature. Describing the confrontation between Rick and Makepeace that took place before his birth, Pym tells of the character Syd is loath to discuss:

> And Rickie, suddenly his gaze has the glint of a flick-knife in the dark. Syd does not go as far as I shall in describing that stare because Syd won't touch the black side of his lifelong hero. But I will. It looks out of him like a child through the eyeholes of a mask. It denies everything it stood for not a half-second earlier. It is pagan. It is amoral. It regrets your decision and your mortality. But it has no choice because you cannot go back.

> Rick's spirits are back, because the flick-knife never shows for long and because he has already achieved the object that is more important to him than any other in his human dealings, even if he himself does not yet know it. He has inspired Makepeace to hold two totally divergent opinions of him and perhaps more. He has shown him the official and unofficial versions of his identity. He has taught him to respect Rick in his complexity and to reckon as much with Rick's secret world as with his overt one.

Throughout the book, Rick is to show official and unofficial versions of himself, frequently at the same time.

Pym, too, has, as Smiley did, too many heads under his hat. In chapter 1, he prepares to write his narrative, promising

> to tell it to all of you who own me, to whom I have given myself with such unthinking liberality. To my handlers and paymasters.

To Mary and all the other Marys. To anyone who had a piece of
me, was promised more and duly disappointed. And to whatever
of myself remained after the great Pym share-out. . . . Whoever
Pym was to you, whoever you are or were, here is the last of
many versions of the Pym you thought you knew.

Incorporated by Rick into dozens of fake companies, dubbed "Sir Magnus"
by Poppy, who tells Mary, "'Really I sometimes think he is entirely put
together from bits of other people,'" Pym is perhaps best described by Kate:
"'He's a shell. . . . All you have to do is find the hermit crab that climbed
into him. Don't look for the truth about him. The truth is what we gave
him of ourselves.'"

A Perfect Spy, however, is the search for the truth about Pym, and that
truth lies, surely, in that doubleness, that ambiguous parcelling out and past-
ing together which is central not only to Pym, but to the novel's whole world.
The nature of the world created here by le Carré has been the focal point of
critical discussions of his work from the time of *Call for the Dead* to the
present. And there is, in fact, remarkable critical consensus about its salient
features and the way le Carré employs his central espionage metaphors. Since
the purpose of this paper, as I stated earlier, is to look more at the agent as
double than at the double agent, I shall confine myself to a brief summary
of some of the more important aspects of le Carré's fictional world.

It is, first of all, the world in which le Carré's novels have always been
set (with the exception of parts of *The Honourable Schoolboy* and *A Little
Drummer Girl*), postwar Britain and Europe. Here is a spy's paradise, the
ideal home for the displaced person, the schizophrenic center for the search
for value, for truth, for identity, both national and individual. Le Carré identified the historical, national crisis of Britain in his introduction to *Philby*:

> Soldiers who had fought at Bastogne were now required to fight
> in Korea. Airmen who had defended London were now required
> to defend Berlin. In Germany itself there were those who were
> taking away and those who were handing back, there were those
> who spoke of the allies and no longer meant the Russians, those
> who spoke of the enemy and no longer meant the Germans.

Britain has lost its political certitude with its political power, but makes up
for that impotence by dedicating itself to self-perpetuation, even when that
self can no longer be defined.

Europe is even more perplexed. The Austria to which Pym is stationed
after leaving Oxford is a divided country: "The Americans had Salzburg as

their capital, the French Innsbruck and the Brits Graz, and everyone had a
piece of Vienna to play with." (Indeed, the British Foreign Office's "one
positive achievement" in Pym's lifetime is that it signed a treaty with the
other countries and left Austria, having, after all, Berlin to squabble over.)
Berlin has the Wall, and as for Poppy's home, Carlsbad, it "was in the
Sudetenland. . . . First it was Austria, then it became Germany. Now it was
Czechoslovakia and had a new name [Carlova Very] and the Germans had
all been chucked out." When even countries have lost their identity, what
hope is there for individuals?

Heroes of le Carré's fiction constantly strain to reconcile contraries.
Enmeshed in the bureaucracy of reason, they seek an anarchy of feeling;
bound to the aims of the group, they pursue solitary desires; dedicating their
faith to an ideal, they helplessly betray a reality. Le Carré finds in the espionage systems of the Cold War the complete microcosm of and metaphor
for the war-weary worlds of Europe. For here in the West is a society which
must destroy individuals to protect individualism and in the East a state
which sacrifices individualism to collective need. Where does the ideal lie?

In *A Perfect Spy,* the perfect loyalty may be found (or at least sought)
in a perfect betrayal:

> Axel was as keen for Pym to love England as he was to direct
> him at America, and it was part of his genius throughout our
> partnership to praise the freedoms of the West while tacitly im-
> plying that Pym had it within his reach, if not his duty as a free
> man, to bring some of this freedom to the East. . . . Can you not
> imagine how easily it came to Pym to take a tiny, impoverished
> country into his protection, when his own was so favoured, so
> victorious and wellborn? And, from where he saw it, so absurd?
> To love poor Czecho like a rich protector through all her terrible
> vicissitudes, for Axel's sake? To forgive her lapses in advance?
> And blame them on the many betrayals that his parent England
> had perpetrated against her? Does it honestly amaze you that
> Pym, by making bonds with the forbidden, should be once more
> escaping from what held him?

Grant Lederer relentlessly tracks down Pym the double agent even as he
affirms his friendship; he seeks Brotherhood's respect as he exposes the
British Secret Service's lies to his own agency. "Quite desperate for Brotherhood's absolution," Lederer explains that: "'I cast aspersions on one of
your men, that's duty. But if I were ever able to separate the personal and
the official sides, I'd be a happy man.'" Even Jack Brotherhood, usually

singleminded in both aims and actions, when Pym's possible duplicity is first mooted to him, storms that: " 'There's not a man or woman in this room who won't look like a traitor once you start to pull our life stories inside out.' "

Each of these men seeks a cohesive identity; an armistice to reconcile his war-torn selves. Ironically, they seek it in a service and a calling which demand fragmentation. For a single goal—Patriotism, Duty, Freedom, Empire, whatever abstract most appeals—the Secret Service calls, not on the singlemindedness of its agents, but on their duplicity, their ability to live several lives at once. After which, it sends them out to divide and conquer.

Grant Lederer, self-proclaimed "howling psychopath," recognizes the way fragmentation has allowed him to pursue a single aim:

> I am the bounty hunter, shuttling between London, Washington and Vienna with Pym perpetually in my sights. . . . The Lederer who for the last twelve months—ever since Pym's name began to wink at me from the computer screen—has tracked him first as an abstraction, then as a fellow screwball. Has posed with him on spurious committees as his earnest and admiring colleague. Shared jolly drunken picnics with family Pym in the Vienna woods, then rushed back to my desk and set to work with fresh vigour to rip apart what I have just enjoyed. I am the Lederer who too easily attaches himself, then punishes whatever holds him tight; the Lederer who is grateful for every wiry smile and casual pat of encouragement from the great Wexler, my master, only to round on him minutes later, lampooning him, degrading him in my overheated mind, punishing him for being yet another disappointment to me.

Betraying to be loyal, Lederer survives by relying on qualified faith: "Somewhere, he argues to himself, there is worth and secrecy and an all-knowing intelligence service. The only trouble is, it's in Heaven." Brotherhood recognizes that "in every operation there is an above the line and a below the line. Above the line is what you do by the book. Below the line is how you do the job." Disillusioned with the men who run the Service, Brotherhood nonetheless commits himself to the group: "Belatedly, and in the teeth of more larcenous instincts, he knew he must conform . . . not out of slavishness but because he believed in the fight and, despite everything, the team."

Perhaps the clearest expression of the Firm's ambiguous faith comes in the last of Pym's many recruitments into it:

The last question of the interview and Pym's answer echo for ever in my head. A military man in tweeds put it.

"Look here, young Pym," he demanded, with a thrust of his bucolic head. "You're by way of being a Czech buff. Speak their language a bit, know their people. What d'you say to these purges and arrests they're having over there? Worry you?"

"I think the purges are quite appalling, sir. But they are to be expected," said Pym, fixing his earnest gaze upon a distant, unreachable star.

"Why *expected*?" demanded the military man, as if nothing ought to be.

"It's a rotten system. It's superimposed on tribalism. It can only survive by the exercise of oppression."

"Yes, yes. Granted. So what would you do about it—*do*?"

"In what capacity, sir?"

"As one of us, you fool. Officer of this service. Anyone can talk. We *do*."

Pym had no need to think. His patent sincerity was out there speaking for him already.

"I'd play their game, sir. I'd divide them against themselves. Spread rumour, false accusation, suspicion. I'd let dog eat dog."

"You mean you wouldn't mind getting innocent chaps chucked into prison by their own police, then? Being a bit harsh, aren't you? Bit immoral?"

"Not if it shortens the life of the system. No, sir, I don't think I am."

And, in joining the Service, Pym finds himself being simultaneously recruited into marriage with Belinda: "That's me taken care of, then, he thought. With the Firm getting one half of me and Belinda the other, I'll never want for anything again."

Mention of marriage brings us to what is in most of le Carré's fiction the main hope, perhaps the only one, for some kind of unity, a way to reconcile opposites of self and circumstance: love. While it rarely saves, love wards off total despair. Leamas of *The Spy Who Came In from the Cold* dies to acknowledge the importance of his love for Liz, as does Jerry Westerby of *The Honourable Schoolboy* in support of his love for Lizzie and of Drake and Nelson Ko's love for each other. Since willing your own murder is hardly a successful way to live, we must recognize the qualified hope love offers. Perhaps the closest le Carré comes to affirming this hope in his books previous to *A Perfect Spy* is the coupling of Charlie and Joseph in *The Little Drummer Girl*. The fulfillment offered in that ending remains problematical, however, for Charlie and Joseph arguably have been destroyed by their experiences: "I'm dead, she kept saying, I'm dead, I'm dead. But it seemed he wanted her dead or alive. Locked together, they set off awkwardly along the pavement, though the town was strange to them."

In *A Perfect Spy*, the chances even love has of unifying a fragmented self, or providing any transcendence to the irreconcilable polarities of reality appear to have vanished. If, in *The Looking Glass War*, love is whatever you can still betray, here betrayal is what posits love. In the one, the emphasis was on the subject, love. In *A Perfect Spy*, betrayal is the subject. Pym writes to Mary: "'If love is whatever we can still betray, remember that I betrayed you on a lot of days.'" What else can be expected in a world where a book entitled *Guidance on Marriage* turns out to be a handbook on mortgages?

These, then, are the dualities which lie at the heart of le Carré's fictional world. What of the psychic ambiguities inherent in le Carré's use of doubled characters? Here it is appropriate to consider that doubling has a temporal as well as a spatial aspect: doubling can also be repetition. And it is with doubling and repetition, with repetition and revenge that I shall now concern myself.

In his brilliant "speculative reading" of William Faulkner, *Doubling and Incest/Repetition and Revenge,* John T. Irwin considers certain major texts of Faulkner in conjunction with texts of Freud, Nietzsche, and Rank. Interestingly, many of his theses apply with singular appositeness to *A Perfect Spy*. (I must make it clear, however, that I shall not attempt to use every one of Irwin's theories, nor, indeed, do I necessarily apply them in exactly the same way as he applies them: le Carré is not Faulkner and *A Perfect Spy* is neither *Absalom, Absalom!* nor *The Sound and the Fury*. Rather, I find in Irwin's book several ideas that seem to me appropriate to a reading of *A Perfect Spy* and le Carré.) In the light of Irwin's observations on doubling and the repetition compulsion, le Carré shows himself writing in *A Perfect Spy* of the son's revenge on the father, and, in writing *A Perfect Spy* as his eleventh novel, he shows his own attempted revenge on Father Time.

Irwin begins by considering repetition and narration; repetition as "the process of discovering the different ways in which one says the same about the Same." He argues:

> The motive force of ... repetitions is, in a very real sense, an
> oblique revenge against time, for if revenge means trying to get
> even, then in light of Freud's economic model for psychic energy

exchanges and the principle of constancy, those repetitions are
attempts to stabilize or equalize a tension, attempts "to get even"
in terms of energy levels for an insult or affront to the psychic
apparatus. But because of the irreversibility of the flow of time,
the insult or affront can never be gotten at directly, and the reversal, the flowing back or discharge of energy that equalizing or
"getting even" demands, always involves an oblique attempt to
get even with that irreversibility of time that has rendered the
original affront immune to direct action. One might say that the
purpose and point of . . . all narration, is to use the temporal
medium of narration to take revenge against time, to use narration to get even with the very mode of narration's existence in a
daemonic attempt to prove that through the process of substitution and repetition, time is not really irreversible.

A *Perfect Spy* is a repetitive novel about repetition; a narrative about narration. The matter of spy fiction, it has been said, is the search for the hunted
man, and so it is here. Brotherhood, Mary, Lederer, and Poppy all look for
Magnus; when he is found, the novel ends. But their search parallels Pym's
search for himself. In alternating sections or chapters, Pym's hunters pursue
him, physically and mentally, and Pym tries to record for Tom the story of
his betrayals, which is the story of his life. Le Carré, in juxtaposing these
narratives, repeats their pursuit, seeking also the man Pym, whose story he
tells achronologically, as a series of betrayals, a series of narratives. Brotherhood, Mary, and Lederer share a double search for Pym, one that is mental
as well as physical. That mental pursuit necessarily becomes, as well, a search
for their own identities, their own self-understanding in the light of Pym's
betrayal. Pym looks for an explanation of himself for himself, and, more
importantly, for Tom; he circles endlessly around the selves he has been,
trying to find or to create a single one to give to Tom as a farewell present.
Le Carré writes a novel which emphasizes repetition, repeating in it his
earlier novels, doubling himself in his text and his hero. In the remainder of
this paper, I shall concentrate on Pym, as both central narrator and a center
of the novel's narration.

What is the "insult or affront to the psychic apparatus" with which
Pym attempts to get even by his repetitions? It seems to be his betrayal of
Axel, a betrayal which becomes the primary scene for Pym, the action which
cannot be repeated in truth (and so, reversed) and therefore must be repeated
in time and in narration. The betrayal of Axel occurs at practically the exact
midpoint of the novel. It is what the book has been leading up to and what

it perpetually looks back on, the explanation of Pym's treachery, his decision
to be a double agent. The primacy of the scene where Jack Brotherhood leads
Pym to betray Axel is attested to by the rest of the narration of *A Perfect
Spy* as well, for it is Pym the double agent, Pym the traitor, who is sought
by Brotherhood, Mary, Lederer, and Poppy. Indeed, every action of Pym's
eventually comes to be seen as some sort of repetition of, or precursor to,
this central action. Pym wills the repetitions, as Nietzsche puts it, in order
to assert the primacy of the will against the irreversibility of time; he writes
of the betrayal, and all the other betrayals, to gain control over them.

Yet, does this constitute the most important betrayal of the book, its
central action? I think not. Rather, Pym's betrayal of Rick, the scene in
Gulworth North where he gives Peggy Wentworth the information from
Rick's filing cabinet, must be Pym's primary betrayal, the one he most tries
to deny. Indeed, Pym's insistence on the centrality of the Axel betrayal shows
a kind of psychic and narrative bluffing; the particular steps by which Pym
became a double agent are not the purpose of the narrative. Who Pym is,
that is the subject of the quest. And Pym is Rick's son and Tom's father; his
betrayal is the revenge of the son on the father for his being first and the
rejection by the father of the revenge of the son. In a very real sense, Pym's
suicide represents his murder of Rick. He complains to himself just before
he describes the by-election and his betrayal of Rick: "Rick should have died
when I killed him." Rick refused to die, but Pym kills himself (while looking
in a mirror, which I'll consider more fully further on in the paper), seeing
himself not only as a substitute for Rick-as-victim, but also for Tom-as-
killer. Pym makes the Axel betrayal the focus of the repetitions, however, in
an attempt to evade his true crime; he accomplishes this through the repetitions he describes; in particular, by the rhetoric of repetition he uses.

After Pym betrays Axel, he experiences feelings exactly parallel to those
he felt when he carved Sefton Boyd's initials on the staff lavatory, his first
betrayal. Compare the two scenes:

> All afternoon he waited, confident nothing had happened. I didn't
> do it. If I went back it wouldn't be there. It was Maggs in third
> form. It was Jameson who owns a kukri, I saw him go in. An
> oik from the village did it, I saw him sneaking round the grounds
> with a dagger in his belt, his name is Wentworth. At evensong
> he prayed that a German bomb would destroy staff lavatory.
> None did. Next day, he presented Sefton Boyd with his greatest
> treasure, the koala bear Lippsie had given him after his appendix
> operation. In break he buried his penknife in the loose earth

behind the cricket pavilion. Or as I would say today, cached it.
It was not until evening line-up that the full name of the Honourable Kenneth Sefton Boyd was called out in a voice of doom
by the duty master, the sadist O'Mally. Mystified, the young no-
bleman was led to Mr. Grimble's study. Mystified himself, Pym
watched him go. Whatever can they want him for—my friend,
my best friend, the owner of my koala bear? The mahogany door
closed, eighty pairs of eyes fixed upon its fine workmanship,
Pym's also. Pym heard Mr. Grimble's voice, then Sefton Boyd's
raised in protest. Then a great silence while God's justice was
administered, blow by blow. Counting, Pym felt cleansed and
vindicated. So it wasn't Maggs, it wasn't Jameson and it wasn't
me. Sefton Boyd did it himself, otherwise he would not have been
beaten.

How Pym loved Axel in the weeks that followed! For a day or
so, it was true, he would not go near him, he resented him so
much. He resented everything about him, every move on the other
side of the radiator. He patronises me. He sneers at my ignorance
without respecting my strengths. He is an arrogant German of
the worst sort and Jack is right to keep his eye on him. Pym
resented the mail he received, Herr Axel care of Ollinger. He
resented more than ever the Marthas tiptoeing like shy disciples
up the stairs to the great thinker's sanctum, and down again two
hours later. He is dissolute. He is unnatural. He is turning their
heads for them, exactly as he tried to turn mine. Diligently he
kept a log of these developments to give to Brotherhood at their
next meeting . . .
     He could tell when Axel could not sleep by the striking of his
matches as he lit his cigars. He could tell when his body was
driving him mad. He told it by the altered rhythm of his movements and the determined gaiety of his singing as he clomped the
wooden corridor to crouch for hours in their shared lavatory with
its porcelain footprints. After several nights had passed that way
Pym was able to loathe Axel for his incontinence. Why doesn't
he go back to hospital? "He sings German marching songs," he
wrote to Brotherhood in his notebook. "Tonight he sang the
whole Horst Wessel Lied in the lavatory." On the third night,
long after Pym had gone to bed, his door suddenly flew open and
there stood Axel wrapped in Herr Ollinger's dressing-gown.

"Well? Have you forgiven me yet?"

"What have I got to forgive you for?" Pym replied, discreetly pushing his secret logbook under the bedclothes.

Axel stayed in the doorway. The dressing-gown was ridiculously large for him. Sweat had made black fangs of his moustache. "Give me some of your priest's whisky," he said.

After that Pym couldn't let Axel go until he had wiped the shadows of suspicion from his face. The weeks passed and spring began and Pym knew that nothing was happening, and that he had never betrayed Axel in the first place, because if he had they would have done something long ago. . . . After that Pym studied and strove for Axel in every way he knew, now denying to himself that Brotherhood existed anywhere but in his mind, now congratulating himself on Axel's continued survival, which was owed entirely to Pym's nimble manipulation of irresistible forces.

.   .   .

They came in the small hours of a spring morning, just when we fear them most: when we want to live the longest and are most afraid of dying. Soon, unless I make their journey unnecessary, they will come for me in the same way. If so, I trust I shall see the justice of it and relish the circularity of life. . . . Pym knew there were three of them because he could count their stealthy Father Christmas footsteps on the squeaky top stair. They looked in the lavatory before they placed themselves outside Axel's door. Pym knew this because he heard the lavatory door squeak and stay open. He also heard a rattle as they removed the lavatory-door key in case their desperate criminal should attempt to lock himself inside. But Pym could do nothing personally because at the time he lay deeply dreaming in all the scared beds of his childhood. He dreamt about Lippsie and her brother Aaron and how he and Aaron together had pushed her off the rooftop at Mr. Grimble's school. He dreamt that an ambulance was waiting outside the house like the one that called at The Glades for Dorothy, and that Herr Ollinger was trying to stop the men coming up the stairs but was being ordered back to his quarters in a fury of Swiss dialect. He dreamt that he heard a shout of "Pym, you bastard, where are you?" from the direction of Axel's room and directly afterwards the awful brief thundering noise of a man with

uneven legs struggling against three healthy intruders and the
furious opposition of Bastl whom Axel had once accused of being
his Faustian Devil. But when he lifted his head from the pillow
and listened to the real world, there was silence and everything
was absolutely fine.

In both betrayals, Pym's reaction is to deny the action, to displace it onto
the victim. In each instance, then, Pym's victim is not only a substitute for
Rick, against whom Pym seeks the true revenge, but is also a substitute for
Pym, the avenger. In Pym's mind, each victim has betrayed himself. Pym
further removes himself from the action by forcing a third person to perform
the revenge Pym himself seeks. Mr. Grimble, standing in for God, beats
Sefton Boyd. The Americans (probably—earlier, Brotherhood had said that
Americans always came in threes, at least), standing in for Brotherhood, take
Axel away to prison. As they take Axel away, Pym thinks of Lippsie's death,
and Dorothy's purgatory, thus connecting them as well to Axel's betrayal.

Pym further substitutes Judy for Rick as victim in his betrayal of Rick.
During the by-election, Pym comes close to his first sexual consummation
with Judy, but concentrates instead on the green filing cabinet, and Rick.
Again, the scene in the basement in Gulworth North where Pym meets Peggy
Wentworth is described in terms of Pym's first meeting with Axel in the
cellar of the Ollinger's house. Listening to Peggy's story, he thinks again of
Lippsie, of Dorothy at The Glades, of himself in an attic in Switzerland
"wondering to God why he has killed his friend to please an enemy." So
Pym ignores his date with Judy to read the material in the filing cabinet. As
Peggy accuses Rick, an agent once more standing in for Pym, Pym concen-
trates on his betrayal of Judy:

> He thought he saw Judy's pale face and big pale eyes behind their
> serious spectacles, watching him from the centre of the crowd.
> My father needed me, he wanted to explain to her. I forgot where
> the bus stop was. I lost your phone number. I did it for my
> country. The Bentley was waiting at the front steps, Cudlove at
> the door. Riding away at Rick's side, Pym imagined he heard
> Judy calling out his name: "Pym. You bastard. Where are you?"

Throughout the book, Pym emphasizes that Poppy/Axel is his nemesis,
his Wentworth. Long before we have reached the scene of Axel's betrayal,
therefore, we see Pym distancing himself from Rick. He and Rick have parallel nemeses; Poppy is to be doubled with Wentworth, not with Rick, in the
language of betrayal. As we have seen, however, Poppy is also a double for

Rick. He becomes simply another substitute for Rick. Pym betrays Poppy first almost as a way of enabling him to betray Rick, the real father. (And if fact does not enable the betrayal, the narrative does.) Despite his rhetorical insistence on the primacy of the Poppy betrayal, Pym himself reveals this when, as he reads the papers in Rick's cabinet, he thinks: "This is what I was born for, if I was born at all. I am God's detective, seeing everybody right."

That the betrayal of Rick should coincide with the sexual failure of Pym lies at the heart of Pym's compulsion to betray and fits in with Irwin's discussion of doubling and incest, castration and impotence. In all his betrayals, Pym forces himself to assume a passive, feminine role. Everyone he betrays is, in his mind, self-betrayed, and is, in fact, punished by another agent. Irwin writes:

> The explanation for [the] shifting from a masculine to a feminine role is to be found in the son's ambivalence toward his father in the castration complex. On the one hand, there is an aggressive reaction of the son toward the castrating father, a desire for the father's death, a desire to kill him. But on the other hand, there is a tender reaction, a desire to renounce the object that has caused the father's anger, to give up the penis and thus to retain the father's love by assuming a passive, feminine role in relation to him—in short, to become the mother in relation to the father. In this second situation (the tender, passive reaction) the fear of castration turns into a longing for castration, and since, as Freud points out, the fear of death is an analogue of the fear of castration, this transformation of the castration fear into a desire for castration within the incest scenario has as its analogue, within the scenario of narcissistic doubling, that fear of death that becomes a longing for death—the paradox, as Rank says, of a thanatophobia that leads to suicide. What the fear of castration is to incest the fear of death is to doubling, and as the fear of castration and the fear of death are analogues, so too are incest and doubling.

Throughout the book, we have seen Pym's desire for the mother; whether it be for Dorothy, his partner at The Glades, or, more explicitly, for Lippsie, Dorothy's double and Rick's mistress. Indeed, his first overtly sexual encounter is the (possibly apocryphal) scene in which he and Lippsie bathe together, of which he persists in remembering nothing after she measures out the bath water. Elena Weber, too, plays the role of desirable mother for

Pym. Pym's first reaction when he meets her is to think: "It's Dorothy. . . . It's Lippsie." Presumably another of Rick's mistresses, E. Weber is another of Pym's sexual failures. Desire for incest, for the mother, leads to fear of the castrating potency of the father. Pym writes to Tom that Rick "gobbled up the natural humanity in him." The image inevitably recalls Kronos devouring his children; Kronos, who castrated his father Ouranos and was in his turn castrated by his son Zeus. (We should recall that Rick took Makepeace Watermaster's woman—the daughter he desired sexually—from him at the beginning of the book.) Betrayal, then, is inextricably bound with sexuality; revenge against the father is the son's search for engendering authority.

This is made explicit in the scene of Pym's betrayal of Rick. For originally the betrayal was to be active. Pym and Judy have agreed that "somewhere around ten-thirty . . . Judy Barker will take Magnus Pym to the barn and annoint him her full and consummated lover." And Pym feels certain that "a man who can gain access to Judy's breasts can burst open the fortress of Rick's secrets." But, as we have seen, at the appointed time for sexual consummation, Pym is involved in Rick's betrayal, and, as he failed Judy, so he fails to attack Rick in person, but assigns Peggy Wentworth to take over. Fear of castration here becomes desire for castration, as Pym assumes the passive, feminine role, and appears at first to rebound on himself. For Rick, having escaped Peggy, confronts Pym in the car after the meeting with the full knowledge of Pym's lies about Oxford. Grasping Pym's hand so tightly he nearly breaks the fingers, Rick unmans as he unmasks Pym, then "wipes away the tears of Pym's rage and impotence."

Perhaps we can now see why Pym substitutes the betrayal of Axel for the betrayal of Rick as engendering scene. The betrayal of Rick, though Pym performs just as he had done in his previous betrayals, doesn't work. Rick does not die when Pym kills him, but rather turns on Pym and attacks. Poppy, who with his potent and assured Rick-like sexuality clearly acts as Rick's double here, disappears. The betrayal is successful. If Pym can make Axel substitute for Rick, then, even the betrayal of Rick becomes in some sense successful; is it not a repetition of the betrayal of Axel? Substituting Judy for Rick in the rhetoric of betrayal highlights the sexual basis of the action; in fact, it makes Rick the passive female, thus reversing the unmanning of Pym into the unmanning of Rick. Furthermore, by assuming the feminine role Pym creates in some sense a double for himself, someone else to suffer the "unmanning." Irwin points out the paradox by which acceptance of castration saves: "By courageously facing the fear of death, the fear of castration, the fear of one's own worst instincts, one slays that fear; by taking the risk of being feminized, by accepting the feminine elements in the self, one establishes one's masculinity." Pym, of course, can hardly be called courageous, and he needs to do some fancy narrative maneuvering to make the scene come right. But that narrative reshaping is itself a kind of doubling. We are given, at the same time, the authorized and the unauthorized versions of the symbolic castration: we are told, within the narrative, what literally happened, and told, by means of the rhetoric with which the narrative is structured, what figuratively Pym wanted to happen.

Nonetheless, contrived as it is, this "killing" of Rick, as we have seen Pym refer to it, finally enables Pym to achieve sexual consummation with Sabina, who is "like E. Weber" and, when she undresses Pym for their first love-making, does so "severely, like Lippsie." Indeed, after his sexual initiation, Pym becomes sexually another Rick, using women like Kate and Mary. Pym sees all his betrayals in the light of the Poppy betrayal, then, because he achieved through that action a chance for an active share in his own life, even though he continues to describe both that betrayal and his later decision to betray Jack and anyone else who stands in the way of his allegiance to Poppy as forced upon him, in effect, because he is Rick's son.

Irwin discusses passive repetition in relation to Freud's consideration of it in his essay on the uncanny. Freud says:

> Thus we have come across people all of whose human relationships have the same outcome. . . . This "perpetual recurrence of the same thing" causes us no astonishment when it relates to *active* behaviour on the part of the person concerned and when we can discern in him an essential character-trait which always remains the same and which is compelled to find expression in a repetition of the same experiences. We are much more impressed by cases where the subject appears to have a *passive* experience, over which he has no influence, but in which he meets with a repetition of the same fatality.

Are Pym's betrayals passive? Certainly he tries to make them so. We have seen the language he uses to evade his responsibility in the beating of Sefton Boyd and the arrest of Poppy. Now let us look at the final decision; the time when he commits himself irrevocably to Poppy. Surely this, at least, will prove an active one—after all, he is here *reversing* betrayal, he is swearing allegiance.

This is the language in which the decision is announced:

> No, Tom. As Pym walked the momentous night away under a canopy of unreachable ideals, eschewing Sabina's bed in his purity

> of soul, he was not tormenting himself over great choices. He was not examining his immortal spirit in anticipation of what purists might call a treasonable act. He did not consider that tomorrow was the day set for his irrevocable execution—the day on which all hope for Pym would die and your father would be born. He was watching the dawn rise on a day of beauty and harmony. A day when a bad record could be put straight, when the fate of everyone he was responsible for rested in his care, when the electors of his secret constituency would go down on their knees and thank Pym and his Maker that he had been born to see them right. He was glowing and exulting. He was letting his goodwill and self-faith fill him up with courage. The secret crusader had placed his sword upon the altar and was transmitting fraternal messages to the God of Battles.

The first part of the paragraph consists entirely of negatives: Pym was not doing anything active in the decision-making. The decision itself becomes the "execution"—Pym is killed so Tom's father can be born. And the birth itself comes with the dawn, and is described entirely by passive verbs. At the same time Pym is dying, however, Rick is being born in Pym's language. Pym walks under a canopy of "unreachable ideals," as Rick, following Makepeace Watermaster, calls the stars; he has been born to see the electors of his constituency right; Rick's eternal promise to his court and to the world. So, Pym's decision, Pym's reincarnation as the new Rick, are passively willed repetitions, at least in Pym's rhetoric. Here, then, we finally must consider the role of writing, the role of narration, in the making of *A Perfect Spy*.

The power of writing, fittingly enough, is attested to in the scene of Poppy's betrayal and arrest. After Poppy has been taken away, Pym muses:

> I held it against you Jack, I confess. . . . Why had you done it to him? He wasn't English, he wasn't a Communist, he wasn't the war criminal the Americans claimed he was. He was nothing to do with you. His only crimes were his poverty, his illegal presence and his lameness—plus a certain freedom in his way of thinking, which in the eyes of some is what we are there to protect. But I did nurse a grudge and I'm sorry. Because now of course I know you hardly gave it a thought. Axel was another bit of barter material. You wrote him up; he came back into your in-tray looking formidable and sinister in Wendy's flawless type.

In "Wendy's flawless type," Axel becomes a dangerous person; a man is what he is perceived to be. "The truth is what we gave him of ourselves." The greatest irony, the real danger, is that Brotherhood's typed report will come true. Because of "Wendy's flawless type," because of Pym's complicity in Axel's arrest, Axel can bind Pym to him forever: "Axel was his keeper and his virtue, he was the altar on which Pym had laid his secrets and his life." "I tell you, Jack: we reap as we sow, even if the harvest is thirty-five summers in the growing." (We might recall here that Pym described the metaphysics of betrayal as loyalty by explaining that he "love[s] poor Czecho . . . for Axel's sake.")

Writing, then, possesses an authority all its own, an authority likely to appeal to a man whose whole life revolves around the question of engendering. Irwin, discussing Quentin Compson's narrative act in *Absalom, Absalom!*, posits:

> Is there no virgin space in which one can be first, in which one can have authority through originality? . . . In light of this question . . . we can gain an insight into Quentin's act of narration in *Absalom*, for what is at work . . . is the question of whether narration itself constitutes a space in which one can be original, whether an "author" possesses "authority," whether that repetition which in life Quentin has experienced as a compulsive fate can be transformed in narration, through an act of the will, into a power, a mastery of time.

Discussing Pym's treachery, Lederer suggests to Brotherhood that "'if Magnus's writing had ever worked for him, he'd have been okay.'" Pym himself sits down to write his narrative to give himself freedom: "To tell it straight, he rehearsed. Word for word the truth. No evasions, no fictions, no devices. Just my overpromised self set free. . . . You do it once. Once in your life and that's it. No rewrites, no polishing, no evasions. No would-it-be-better-this-ways. You're the male bee. You do it once, and die."

But of course he doesn't tell it straight. His very repeating of the promise "no evasions" tells us that evasion will mark the course of the narrative. And from the very beginning, it does. For at once he starts writing of himself in the third person. "But I am running ahead already, for Pym on this particular day was not yet born." Pym is to refer to himself continually in the third person throughout the narrative, but always with an occasional "I" to distinguish and distance himself from Pym. We saw already how, at the moment of decision, Pym died, and Tom's father was born—again, "Tom's father," not "I." Pym is not only creating text to be a double of himself, then, but is creating a double for himself within that text. He rehearses, indeed, creates the repetitions of his life, but he assigns them to "Pym."

As Irwin points out, however, repetition is the result of three distinct actions: the first act, the repeated act, and the most important act—recollection.

> If an action that has been performed once is repeated and the previous occurrence is remembered, then the second performance of that action reconstitutes the previous performance as the first time—reconstitutes it as the first time not just by the act of repeating it but by a third action, an act of recollection, in which the second action and the first action are seen as related.

For Pym, that recollection takes the form of narration. And that narration *creates* the events, for it defines the repetitions. In forcing primacy on the wrong betrayal, as we have seen, the narrative becomes an attempt to remake the events, to leave, out of time, a record which will change time, and give it into Pym's control.

Does Pym's writing "work for him," then? We have seen the power narrative has to make reality in the case of "Wendy's flawless type" and Axel's arrest. We have seen Pym reconstructing himself as passive victim of the repetition of betrayal. He has created a double of Rick to kill, and a double of Rick to castrate to escape the truth of Rick's remaining alive and his own impotence. But we must return to the novel's first question and first subject: the identity of Magnus Pym.

Pym fails in his narrative search because he cannot find his voice. A divided person may still have a single voice—Rick's is unmistakable (although we must not forget that the only person who ever talks for Rick is Pym)—but Pym is a "mimic." His voice is compounded of Rick's voice, and Syd's voice, Poppy's and Brotherhood's, and the hundreds of people he meets along the way. In the course of a single sentence he can be the "I" who writes to Tom, and Pym, and Ollie and Cudlove all talking about socialism:

> And though political doctrines are at root as meaningless to me today as they were to Pym then, I remember the simple humanity of our discussions as we promised to mend the world's ills, and the truthful goodheartedness with which, as we went off to bed, we wished each other peace in the spirit of Joe Stalin who, let's face it, Titch, and nothing against your dad *ever,* won the war for all these capitalist bastards.

In his search for narrative control, then, Pym betrays the man who sits down to write. And in this, I think, we can see the importance of his insistence on doing it "once" and then dying. A lifetime of repetition will lead only to death.

Here, Irwin's gloss on Freud may prove illuminating. Irwin considers Freud's statement about the uncanniness of the apparent passive repetition, which seems to be instinctual:

> What does it mean to say that the compulsion to repeat is "instinctual," thus locating it on the level of the primary process of the unconscious and its unbound energy? Freud's answer turns the question around, for he suggests that the repetition compulsion is a "universal attribute of instincts." Thus, it is not so much that the compulsion to repeat is instinctual as that the very essence of the instincts is the compulsion to repeat. He asserts that *"an instinct is an urge inherent in organic life to restore an earlier state of things* which the living entity has been obliged to abandon under the pressure of external disturbing forces; . . ." Instincts are "an expression of the *conservative* nature of living substance." From this he concludes that the final goal of all organic striving, the ultimate earlier state which the instincts attempt to restore, is that inanimate condition from which all animate life sprang: "If we are to take it as a truth that knows no exception that everything living dies for *internal* reasons—becomes inorganic once again—then we shall be compelled to say that '*the aim of all life is death.*'"

(Consider, in the light of this theory, Lederer's explanation to Brotherhood of why so many double agents redefect, as we know Pym in some way to be doing, since he is evading both Brotherhood and Poppy, and intending with his narrative to betray them both. Lederer says: "'Know why so many defectors redefect? . . . It's in and out of the womb all the time. Have you ever noticed that about defectors—the one common factor in all that crazy band? They're immature. Forgive me, they are *literally* mother-fuckers.'") Freud, and Irwin, go on to point out that the death drive encompasses within itself such apparently life-conserving instincts as self-preservation, self-assertion, and mastery. The only true opposite to the death drive is the sex drive, the sexual instincts which are also conservative:

> "They bring back earlier states of living substance; but they are conservative to a higher degree in that they are peculiarly resis-

tant to external influences; and they are conservative too in another sense in that they preserve life itself for a comparatively
long period. They are the true life instincts. They operate against
the purpose of the other instincts, which leads, by reason of their
function, to death. . . . It is as though the life of the organism
moved with a vacillating rhythm. One group of instincts rushes
forward so as to reach the final aim of life as swiftly as possible;
but when a particular stage in the advance has been reached, the
other group jerks back to a certain point to make a fresh start
and so prolong the journey." What characterizes the life instincts
and the death instincts in terms of the compulsion to repeat [says
Irwin] is that they both seek through repetition to restore an
earlier state which has been lost.

Peculiarly appropriate, then, is Pym's reference to narrative as being
analogous to the male bee's sexual act: "You're the male bee. You do it once,
and die." For just as his life has been progressing in a series of repetitions
toward death, so now his narrative, sexually delaying death in the temporality of its composition, nonetheless inexorably drives Pym to his suicide.

During the last chapter, Pym hurries to finish his story, even as the
police line up outside to attack him. What delays them is the gun in the
burn box. Not knowing how many of them Pym may manage to kill before
they disarm or kill him, they wait. The gun, then, is like the narrative—it
delays death, while inexorably forcing death. When the narrative is complete,
Pym goes into the bathroom and looks into the mirror. His suicide will be
a murder as well, the murder, finally, of Pym, of the "perfect spy," who did
not even create himself:

> "What I am saying is, Sir Magnus: for once nature has produced
> a perfect match. You are a perfect spy. . . . All the junk that made
> you what you are: the privileges, the snobbery, the hypocrisy, the
> churches, the schools, the fathers, the class systems, the historical
> lies, the little lords of the countryside, the little lords of big busi-
> ness, and all the greedy wars that result from them, we are sweep-
> ing that away for ever. For your sake. Because we are making a
> society that will never produce such sad little fellows as Sir Mag-
> nus."

Perhaps, as the narrative was the failed attempt to find a voice, to find Pym,
the murderous suicide of the double he has not even created is a last attempt
to gain control: to create the self by killing the self, to revenge himself against

time by putting himself outside of time. He tells Tom, " 'I am the bridge. . . . I am what you must walk over to get from Rick to life.' " The son has finally killed the father, in the hope of giving life to another son. As he pulled the trigger, Pym "noticed how he was leaning: not away from the gun, but into it, like someone a little deaf, straining for a sound."

A Perfect Spy, although a story about Pym, is not a story *by* Pym. I should like, briefly, to consider now John le Carré, and his relation to the narrative, and to the doublings and repetitions involved in writing eleven novels over the past twenty-five years.

Throughout this paper, I have been noting similarities of theme and content among le Carré's novels. From *Call for the Dead* to *A Perfect Spy,* le Carré has written narratives which in major ways duplicate each other—indeed, David Monaghan, at the end of his fine 1985 study of le Carré's fiction, asserts: "The present study of John le Carré's fiction, with its emphasis on recurring elements of theme and technique, should provide a basis for understanding not only the novels with which it deals but also those still unwritten." What compels an author to rewrite his fiction?

Once again, Irwin provides a possible answer. Writing of Faulkner's incessant rewriting of the tale of Quentin Compson, his double, Irwin says that Quentin evokes

> Faulkner's apparent sense of the act of writing as a progressive dismemberment of the self in which parts of the living subject are cut off to become objectified in language, to become (from the writer's point of view) detached and deadened, drained, in that specific embodiment, of their obsessive emotional content. In this process of piecemeal self-destruction, the author, the living subject, is gradually transformed into the detached object—his books. And this process of literary self-dismemberment is the author's response to the threat of death; it is a using up, a consuming of the self in the act of writing in order to escape from that annihilation of the self that is the inevitable outcome of physical generation, to escape by means of an ablative process of artistic creation in which the self is worn away to leave only a disembodied voice on the page to survive the writer's death, a voice that represents the interruption of a physical generative power and the transmission, through the author's books, of the phallic generative power of the creative imagination.

Le Carré, then, seeks through narrative to escape time, to father a text, and to displace into that text the emotional content of experience. It is in his last novel, the first in which he gives himself a clear authorial double, that we can begin to understand specifically what generates his work.

When *The Little Drummer Girl* came out, le Carré gave an interview to Alexis Gelber and Edward Behr of *Newsweek* in which he talked at some length about his childhood and his father, Ronnie. He declared then, ruefully, that although Ronnie had dominated his life, he was still unable to write about him. And, indeed, even in the interviews he has given over the years, we can see Ronnie gradually taking shape in modified repetitions. In the earlier interviews, Ronnie is described as a "Micawber" figure; improvident, to be sure, but built into the Micawber allusion is the le Carré illusion—that Ronnie's improvidence was not criminal, not really shameful, more the result of bad luck and innocence of the world. In 1977, two years after Ronnie's death, le Carré spoke with more openness to Dean Fischer of *Time*; here he admitted that his father had indeed been actively involved in fraud, and, so, not much around to be a father. But then in 1980, in an interview with Marion Gross of the *Observer,* le Carré was once more describing his father in terms of the Micawber figure: "He was a fantasist, perhaps a schizophrenic. . . . A lot of people found him magical, and as a boy, I suppose I did too." His dishonesty? Dismissed with a rueful: "[My brother and I] *had* to go to public school, willy nilly. For this my father always said that he was prepared to steal if necessary; and I'm afraid he did." In *The Little Drummer Girl* interview, however, the Ronnie of the *Time* interview reappears, drawn in greater and more powerful detail. This man is a major criminal, a man who has been arrested for embezzling, who spends other people's money if he spends money at all, but frequently gets by on credit. This is the man le Carré "can't write about," although he admits that he has to some extent incorporated his sister Charlotte into his heroine Charlie.

When *A Perfect Spy* came out, le Carré gave one interview, to Joseph Lelyveld of *The New York Times*. In it, he claimed that he had at last left his fictional father-surrogate, Smiley, to tackle in his fiction his true father, Ronnie. And, in the course of the interview, he does indeed describe a Ronnie with Rick's voice, Rick's mannerisms, and Rick's grand-scale chicanery (for example, one of the favorite stories of le Carré's brother Anthony is the tale of how Ronnie talked himself out of an enormous bill at a hotel by offering to buy the place; in chapter 6 of *A Perfect Spy,* "St. Moritz is off the map following Rick's unsuccessful bid to buy the resort as a substitute for paying his bills there"). What is the significance of Rick-as-Ronnie, Pym-as-le Carré?

I think that *A Perfect Spy* represents the latest in a series of attempts to narrate and so control the circumstances of le Carré's life and generation.

Call for the Dead, and all the other Smiley narratives displaced the father, Ronnie, into the idealized father, Smiley. It is noteworthy that in these novels there was no one who obviously was le Carré's surrogate as son. Guillam, Leamas, and Westerby may have been in some sense Smiley's children, but they were poor doubles for le Carré. Rather, Smiley himself, with his interest in seventeenth-century German literature and his creative power (in *Tinker, Tailor,* for example, he orders the events of the novel, for they arrange themselves largely around his memory and his mental processes) is le Carré's double, even as he is his father. For the first time, in *A Perfect Spy,* we have a clear, authorial double for the author, a son who is also a father. (Leamas had children, but they are totally ignored, by him and everyone else in the book.) Le Carré is finally trying to engender his own father, as well as engender himself, to control his life with his control of the text. (It is also telling that in *A Perfect Spy* le Carré has reduced his own four sons to one son, and made himself an only child in Pym, while le Carré has a brother, and a half-brother and sister.)

To do this, as we saw in Pym's parallel problem, le Carré must find a voice, "a voice that represents the interruption of a physical generative power and the transmission, through the author's books, of the phallic generative power of the creative imagination." Whether le Carré finds his remains, at present, debatable (or, at least, debated). For, like Pym, le Carré is a perfect "mimic." He can do voices; he can give you Pym or Mary or Charlie or Smiley; he can even give you Graham Greene or Joseph Conrad. (Pym's suicide, in which he is described as "straining for a sound" inevitably, and according to Harold Bloom, unfortunately, evokes Decoud's suicide, in *Nostromo,* where Decoud dies, "without having heard the cord of silence snap.") On the whole, though, I feel the mimicry is part of the voice, part of the distinctiveness. Certainly a single style dominates all the books: dry, detached, and ironic, certainty practically absent, sometimes descending into sentimentality and bathos. The early novels, it is true, were narratively straightforward—rarely did they deviate from the omniscient third-person narrator. From the time of *Tinker, Tailor,* however, le Carré's voice has become noticeably more tenuous, as the nature of the reality he wishes to present appears more ambiguous. Thus, even when, in a book like *The Honourable Schoolboy,* he uses a blunt, third-person omniscient narrator, he qualifies our acceptance of that narrator's authority. So we have introjections into the text like this:

> It has been whispered once or twice by certain trivial critics of
> George Smiley that at this juncture he should somehow have seen

> which way the wind was blowing with Jerry, and hauled him out of the field. . . . Had George been at his peak, they say, instead of half-way down the other side, he would have read the warning signals. . . . They might just as well have complained that he was a second-rate fortune-teller.

Although it purports to clear Smiley of any suspicion of mismanagement, the very fact that it admits there is a case to be answered leaves that answer in some doubt. In such a narrative atmosphere, in such a world, the imitating of other voices becomes a way of presenting an uncertain reality. We cannot trust any one voice, not even the author's, for he is a perfect mimic.

Pym wrote: "You do it once, and die." After he finishes his narrative, he commits suicide. Le Carré has, at last count, done it eleven times, and he is still very much alive. For the last time, we shall let Irwin help supply the answer: "When Julius Wiseman [a character in Faulkner's *Mosquitoes*] says '. . . you don't commit suicide when you are disappointed in love. You write a book,' he . . . is telling only part of the truth. For writing a book, creating a work of art, is not so much an alternative to suicide as a kind of alternative suicide: writing as an act of autoerotic self-destruction." For, in the fragmenting of himself into his double, the text, and into his doubles in the text, le Carré throws down pieces to shore up his defense against, and revenge upon, time.

Chronology

<table>
<tr><td>1931</td><td>David John Moore Cornwell born on October 19, in Poole, Dorset. He is the second son of Ronald and Olive Cornwell.</td></tr>
<tr><td>1934–35</td><td>Ronald Cornwell sentenced to two years' imprisonment for fraud. Soon after, Olive Cornwell leaves the family.</td></tr>
<tr><td>1948</td><td>David Cornwell leaves Sherborne School, where he has been studying (he was previously educated at St. Andrew's Preparatory School in Pangbourne). Goes to Bern, where he studies at the University for a year.</td></tr>
<tr><td>1950–52</td><td>Cornwell drafted for national service; joins the army intelligence corps and is posted in Vienna with the British Army of occupation. Involved with the resettlement of refugees; possibly also involved in espionage.</td></tr>
<tr><td>1952–56</td><td>Attends Lincoln College, Oxford, where he reads modern languages. After his father's bankruptcy, withdraws for a year to earn money by teaching at Millfield, but graduates with first-class honors in 1956.</td></tr>
<tr><td>1954</td><td>Ronald Cornwell, now married to the second of his three wives, and father of two more children, Charlotte and Rupert, suffers spectacular bankruptcy. David Cornwell marries Alison Ann Veronica Sharp, daughter of an R.A.F. air marshal, by whom he has three sons.</td></tr>
<tr><td>1956–58</td><td>Cornwell teaches German at Eton College.</td></tr>
<tr><td>1958–60</td><td>Doing freelance illustrating; probably also working for M.I.5 (the British Security Service), under Maxwell Knight, whose book Talking Birds (1961) he illustrates.</td></tr>
</table>

1960–63	Employed by the Foreign Office; posted in Bonn as second secretary at the British Embassy; probably also working for M.I.6 (Secret Intelligence Service).
1961	Publishes *Call for the Dead* under the name John le Carré, since Foreign Office employees are not allowed to publish under their own names.
1962	Publishes *A Murder of Quality*.
1963–64	Posted as consul in Hamburg. Publishes *The Spy Who Came In from the Cold*, which is an immediate bestseller. Le Carré leaves the Foreign Office to devote himself to writing. Receives British Crime Novel Award (1963) and Somerset Maugham Award (1964).
1965	Publishes *The Looking Glass War*. Works on the highly successful film of *The Spy Who Came In from the Cold*, which stars Richard Burton. Receives Edgar Allan Poe Award.
1968	Publishes *A Small Town in Germany*.
1971	Publishes *The Naive and Sentimental Lover*, his only non-espionage novel to date, and a critical and commercial failure. Divorces Ann Cornwell.
1972	Marries Valerie Jane Eustace, editor, by whom he has one son.
1974	Publishes *Tinker, Tailor, Soldier, Spy*.
1975	Ronald Cornwell dies.
1977	Publishes *The Honourable Schoolboy*.
1979	Works on television adaptation of *Tinker, Tailor, Soldier, Spy*, which stars Alec Guinness.
1980	Publishes *Smiley's People*, which he also helps adapt for television.
1982	*The Quest for Karla* published, comprising *Tinker, Tailor, Soldier, Spy*, *The Honourable Schoolboy*, and *Smiley's People*.
1983	Publishes *The Little Drummer Girl*.
1986	Publishes *A Perfect Spy*.

Contributors

HAROLD BLOOM, Sterling Professor of the Humanities at Yale University, is the author of *The Anxiety of Influence, Poetry and Repression,* and many other volumes of literary criticism. A MacArthur Prize Fellow, he is general editor of five series of literary criticism published by Chelsea House.

STEFAN KANFER is Senior Editor of *Time* magazine, and the author of *The International Garage Sale.*

ANDREW RUTHERFORD is the author of two studies of Byron, *Prisons and the Process of Justice: The Reductionist Challenge* and *The Literature of War.*

LeROY L. PANEK teaches in the English Department at Western Maryland College in Westminster. He is the author of *Watteau's Shepherds: The Detective Novel in Britain 1914–1940* and *The Special Branch: The Spy Novel from 1890 to 1980.*

ABRAHAM ROTHBERG is Professor of English at St. John Fisher College. He writes both criticism and fiction.

HOLLY BETH KING is a freelance writer-editor.

HELEN S. GARSON is Professor of English at George Mason University, and the author of *Truman Capote.*

GLENN W. MOST is Assistant Professor of Classics at Princeton University, and co-editor of *The Poetics of Murder.*

LARS OLE SAUERBERG teaches in the English Department at Odense University in Denmark. He is the author of *Secret Agents in Fiction: Ian Fleming, John le Carré and Len Deighton* and co-author of *The Practice of Literary Criticism.*

WILLIAM F. BUCKLEY, JR., is an author, columnist, editor, and television host. He has written numerous books, including *God and Man at Yale* and several spy novels.

DAVID MONAGHAN is Professor of English at Mount Saint Vincent University in Halifax, Nova Scotia. He is the editor of *Jane Austen in a Social Context* and the author of *Jane Austen: Structure and Social Vision* and *The Novels of John le Carré*.

SUSAN LAITY is Associate Editor at Chelsea House Publishers, and a freelance critic. She has written on Vera Brittain, W. S. Gilbert, and nineteenth-century drama.

Bibliography

Alvarez, A. "Half Angels versus Half Devils." *The Observer,* 3 February 1980, 39.

Annan, Noel. "Underground Men." *The New York Review of Books,* 29 May 1986, 3–7.

Atkins, John. *The British Spy Novel: Styles in Treachery.* New York: Riverrun Press, 1984.

Auburn, Mark S. "The Pleasures of Espionage Fiction." *Clues* 4, no. 2 (1983): 30–42.

Barzun, Jacques. "Meditations on the Literature of Spying." *American Scholar* 34 (1965): 167–78.

Binyon, T. J. "A Gentleman among Players." *Times Literary Supplement,* 9 September 1977, 1069.

———. "Theatre of Terror." *Times Literary Supplement,* 25 March 1983, 289.

Broyard, Anatole. "Le Carré's People." *New York Times Book Review,* 13 March 1983, 23.

Burgess, Anthony. "Peking Drugs, Moscow Gold." *New York Times Book Review,* 25 September 1977.

Calendrillo, Linda T. "Cloaks and More Cloaks: Pynchon's *V.* and the Classic Spy Novel." *Clues* 5, no. 2 (1984): 58–65.

———. "Role Playing and 'Atmosphere' in Four Modern British Spy Novels." *Clues* 3, no. 1 (1982): 111–19.

Caute, David. "It Was a Man." *New Statesman,* 8 February 1980, 209.

Dawson, Harry D. "John le Carré's Circus." *The Armchair Detective* 13 (1980): 150.

Diamond, Julie. "Spies in the Promised Land." *Race and Class* 25 (Spring 1984): 35–40.

Finger, Louis. "The Manly One." *New Statesman,* 23 September 1977, 414–15.

Gadney, Reg. "Triple Agents?" *London Magazine* 14, no. 4 (1974): 73–77.

Gillespie, Robert. "The Recent Future: Secret Agents and the Cold War." *Salmagundi* 13 (1970): 45–60.

Grella, George. "Murder and Loyalty." *The New Republic,* 31 July 1976, 23–25.

Halperin, John. "Between Two Worlds: The Novels of John le Carré." *The South Atlantic Quarterly* 79 (1980): 17–37.

James, Clive. "Go Back to the Cold!" *The New York Review of Books,* 27 October 1977, 29–30.

Jeffares, A. Norman. "John le Carré." In *Contemporary Novelists,* edited by James Vinson, 381–82. 3rd ed. London: Macmillan, 1982.

Keating, H. R. F. *Whodunit?: A Guide to Crime, Suspense and Spy Fiction.* New York: Van Nostrand Reinhold, 1982.

King, Holly Beth. "George Smiley—The Reluctant Hero." *Clues* 2, no. 1 (1981): 70–76.

Laqueur, Walter. "Le Carré's Fantasies." *Commentary* 75, no. 6 (1983): 62–67.

Leavis, L. R., and J. M. Blom. "Current Literature, 1977." *English Studies* 59 (1978): 447.

Le Carré, John. "To Russia, with Greetings." *Encounter* 26, no. 5 (1966): 3–6.

Lewis, Peter. *John le Carré.* New York: Frederick Ungar, 1985.

McCormick, Donald. *Who's Who in Spy Fiction.* London: Elm Tree Books, 1977.

Maddox, Tom. "Spy Stories: The Life and Fiction of John le Carré." *The Wilson Quarterly* 10, no. 4 (1986): 158–70.

Merry, Bruce. *Anatomy of the Spy Thriller.* Montreal: McGill-Queen's University Press, 1977.

Monaghan, David. "John le Carré and England: A Spy's-Eye View." *Modern Fiction Studies* 29, no. 3 (1983): 569–82.

———. *The Novels of John le Carré.* Oxford: Basil Blackwell, 1985.

Morris, Donald R. "[Spy Jargon]." *Verbatim* 9, no. 2 (1984): 3–5.

Noland, Richard W. "The Spy Fiction of John le Carré." *Clues* 1, no. 2 (1980): 54–70.

Palmer, Jerry. *Thrillers: Genesis and Structure of a Popular Genre.* New York: St. Martin's, 1979.

Paulin, Tom. "National Myths: Recent Fiction." *Encounter* 54 (June 1980): 58–60.

Prawer, S. S. "The Circus and Its Conscience." *Times Literary Supplement,* 8 February 1980, 131–32.

Prescott, Peter S. "In the Theater of the Real." *Newsweek,* 7 March 1983, 72–73.

Pritchett, V. S. "A Spy Romance." *The New York Review of Books,* 7 February 1980, 22.

Rosenthal, T. G. "Thrillers into Novels." *New Statesman,* 8 November 1968, 641.

Sauerberg, Lars Ole. *Secret Agents in Fiction: Ian Fleming, John le Carré and Len Deighton.* London: Macmillan, 1984.

Symons, Julian. *Mortal Consequences: A History—From the Detective Story to the Crime Novel.* New York: Harper & Row, 1972.

"Wishful Thinking." *Times Literary Supplement,* 24 September 1971, 1138.

Wolcott, James. "The Secret Sharers." *The New York Review of Books,* 14 April 1983, 19–21.

Acknowledgments

" 'Our Impudent Crimes': *The Honourable Schoolboy*" (originally entitled "The Spy Who Came In for the Gold") by Stefan Kanfer from *Time,* 3 October 1977, © 1977 by Time, Inc. Reprinted by permission of TIME. All rights reserved.

"The Spy as Hero: Le Carré and the Cold War" by Andrew Rutherford from *The Literature of War: Five Studies in Heroic Virtue* by Andrew Rutherford, © 1978 by Andrew Rutherford. Reprinted by permission of Macmillan Press Ltd. and Barnes & Noble Books, Totowa, New Jersey.

"Espionage Fiction and the Human Condition" (originally entitled "John le Carré [1931–]") by LeRoy L. Panek from *The Special Branch: The British Spy Novel, 1890–1980* by LeRoy L. Panek, © 1981 by Bowling Green University Popular Press. Reprinted by permission. The notes have been omitted.

"The Decline and Fall of George Smiley: John le Carré and English Decency" by Abraham Rothberg from *Southwest Review* 66, no. 4 (Autumn 1981), © 1981 by Southern Methodist University Press. Reprinted by permission.

"Child's Play in John le Carré's *Tinker, Tailor, Soldier, Spy*" by Holly Beth King from *Clues: A Journal of Detection* 3, no. 2 (Fall/Winter 1982), © 1982 by Pat Browne. Reprinted by permission.

"Enter George Smiley: Le Carré's *Call for the Dead*" by Helen S. Garson from *Clues: A Journal of Detection* 3, no. 2 (Fall/Winter 1982), © 1982 by Pat Browne. Reprinted by permission.

"The Hippocratic Smile: John le Carré and the Traditions of the Detective Novel" by Glenn W. Most from *The Poetics of Murder: Detective Fiction and Literary Theory,* edited by Glenn W. Most and William W. Stowe, © 1983 by Glenn W. Most and William W. Stowe. Reprinted by permission of Glenn W. Most, William W. Stowe, and Harcourt Brace Jovanovich, Inc.

"Fear of Extremes: England's Relationship with Germany and America" (originally entitled "John le Carré: The Enemy Within") by Lars Ole Sauerberg from *Secret Agents in Fiction: Ian Fleming, John le Carré and Len Deighton* by Lars Ole Sauerberg, © 1984 by Lars Ole Sauerberg. Reprinted by permission of Macmillan Press Ltd. and St. Martin's Press, Inc.

"Terror and a Woman: *The Little Drummer Girl*" (originally entitled "Terror and a Woman") by William F. Buckley, Jr., from *The New York Times Book Review,* 13 March 1983, © 1983 by The New York Times Company. Reprinted by permission.

"'A World Grown Old and Cold and Weary': Description as Metaphor" (originally entitled "'A World Grown Old and Cold and Weary': Description as Metaphor in le Carré's Novels") by David Monaghan from *The Novels of John le Carré: The Art of Survival* by David Monaghan, © 1985 by David Monaghan. Reprinted by permission of the author and Basil Blackwell Ltd.

"'The Second Burden of a Former Child': Doubling and Repetition in *A Perfect Spy*" by Susan Laity, © 1987 by Susan Laity. Published for the first time in this volume. Printed by permission.

Index